*Social Change
in a Hostile Environment*

Princeton Studies on the Near East

Social Change
in a Hostile Environment

The Crusaders' Kingdom
of Jerusalem

BY AHARON BEN-AMI

Princeton University Press
Princeton, New Jersey
1969

Copyright © 1969 by Princeton University Press
ALL RIGHTS RESERVED
Library of Congress Catalogue Card: 68-27412

Publication of this book has been
aided by a grant from the
Whitney Darrow Publication Reserve Fund
of Princeton University Press

This book has been set in Baskerville type.

Printed in the United States of America
by Princeton University Press

Preface

The central idea of this book is that societies in conflict tend to respond to one another with structural changes, and that this phenomenon is essential for the understanding of social change.

Sociologists know a good deal about the ways in which individuals are influenced by the institutional frameworks within which they interact. They know much less about how these frameworks are influenced by the international environment. They know more about the role of cultural diffusion in the evolution of individual societies than about how the problems of coping with inter-societal conflict contribute to social change. In other words, they know much about how societies adopt solutions to problems from one another, but little about how, by introducing problems and challenges into one another's system, they induce innovations within their separate structures.

The case of the Crusaders' Kingdom of Jerusalem has special experimental value because here history itself kept social structure constant while varying the international factor. This is a case of the transplantation of a politically organized community from one inter-societal environment to a distinctly different one, showing how social structure was influenced by the new type of international relations, and how its eventual collapse was due almost entirely to a failure to adapt the suddenly irrelevant feudal institutions to meet the challenges of the new international system. Our findings, however, are not thereby limited in their experimental value to transplanted societies. For, in our times especially, a society does not have to migrate in order to find itself in a completely transformed system of international relations. Thus social change is related to inter-societal relations in general, and to the interlockage of conflicting societies in particular.

This work, hopefully a contribution to historical sociology, is organized on a strict one-to-one ratio. That is, each

PREFACE

analytical chapter is preceded by a historical chapter which gives only the facts of the period under examination. This method allows the reader to separate fact from analysis with ease. It also enables him to check back and forth, agreeing or disagreeing with the theoretical elaborations on the basis of the nearby description.

My acknowledgments go first to all the great historians, ancient and modern, whose works have provided me with both fact and inspiration. I am very grateful to Miss Carolyn Andersen, who kindly volunteered to type and retype the manuscript with editorial attention, and to whose labors the index is owed. May I also express my gratitude to Miss Lalor Cadley of Princeton University Press, whose editing and suggestions greatly enhanced the final form of this book.

Aharon Ben-Ami
Jerusalem

January 1969

Contents

Preface		v
Maps	21, 78,	149
I Crusader States about 1130		21
II Crusader States at the Height of Their Power		78
III Empire of Salah-ad-Din		149

1. INTER-SOCIETAL RELATIONS

Introduction	3
A Case Study with Experimental Value	14

2. HISTORICAL INTERLOCKAGE

The Meeting of Normans and Saljuqs in the Middle East	20
The Byzantine Perspective	23
The Perspective of the Italian Maritime Cities	26
The Perspective of the Roman Catholic Church	27
The Saljuqid and Syrian Perspectives	30
The Egyptian Fatimid Perspective	33
The Establishment of Crusaders' Principalities	35
Precarious Interlockage of the Kingdom of Jerusalem	38

3. INSTITUTIONAL LAG AND INNOVATIVE FUNCTIONS

Institutionally Known Ways of Meeting Political Necessities	47
Two Phases of Inter-societal Existence	49
Tendencies and Resistance to Institutional Change	60
Inter-societal System and Social Structure	71

4. CRITICAL TURNING POINTS

Reasons for Encirclement and Isolation of the Latins	77

CONTENTS

The Damascus-Jerusalem Alliance and the Containment of Zangi ... 81
The Alienation of Byzantium and the Fall of Edessa ... 85
From the Second Crusade to the Unification of Moslem Syria ... 93
The Revolution in the Balance of Power ... 107

5. INTERNATIONAL SYSTEMS AND INDUCED FUNCTIONS

Effects of a Changing International Environment ... 118
Cultural Contact and Diffusion ... 121
Applying Past Culture to a New Situation ... 124
Institutionally Unanticipated Functions ... 127
Coping with International Conflict ... 129

6. THE COLLAPSE OF THE KINGDOM

Manpower Deficiency and Social Structure ... 148
Islamic Solidarity under Salah-ad-Din ... 150
Feudal Demoralization ... 159
O' God, the Heathen Came into Thine Inheritance ... 169

7. CONCLUSIONS

Social Structure and Change in an Inter-societal Context ... 178
Stratification and Functions of Political Leadership ... 180
Fusion of Divergent Social Roles as a Form of Social Change ... 182
Characteristics of a Conflict System ... 184
Characteristics of Inter-societal Systems ... 186

Selected Bibliography ... 189

Index ... 191

*Social Change
in a Hostile Environment*

Inter-societal Relations

Introduction

This case study does not employ a "closed" conceptual system of social structure. On the contrary, it aims at finding some essential characteristics of societies through empirical observations. But, as is always the case, empirical observations themselves are "structured." That is, they stem from a definite interest in the solution of some problem, guided by some reasonable hypotheses about the nature and form of the solution. Hence, the impossibility of plunging into the realm of facts and just letting them speak for themselves. They do not speak, but only return the echo of definite thoughts. Yet this echo is perhaps the only sign we have of the relationship of our thoughts to reality. Now, in saying that structured thought precedes experience or experiment, we are only referring to the need for having a destination, a sense of direction, and sails adjusted to the wind accordingly. "No wind serves the ship that has no port of destination," says Montaigne.

A vacuum seems to exist between two extreme modes of thinking about societies. On the one hand, we still retain in some form or another the heritage of the "great pioneers" in sociology who ventured to build vast nets to catch the whole fish of history or evolution.[1] On the other hand, we get more and more perplexed by the high birth rate of a variety of sardine-like "social-systems-in-equilibrium," all "boundary-maintaining" and directionless.

[1] Borrowing an expression from P. Sorokin: "Let the kind and size of fish you want to catch determine the kind and size of net" (Charles P. and Zona K. Loomis, *Modern Social Theories* [Van Nostrand, 1961], p. 591).

CHAPTER 1

The gap between these polar perspectives may provoke a number of ideas. The following one is most relevant to the present study. Supposing one attempts to regard systems of related societies, mutually affecting one another's structure. Would that be an arbitrary intellectual construction or a "real thing"? What would such a complex system look like? Could it suggest a link, however weak at first, between the above-mentioned modes of thinking?

In the first place, this view does not seem arbitrary with regard to our own times. In fact, it is highly unrealistic to try to understand today any individual society (by conventional definition) apart from its conjunctive and disjunctive interaction with other societies. No contemporary culture consists of purely original elements; no economy is completely self-sufficient; no political unit is independent of some international system of cooperation or conflict. Whether we consider the so-called underdeveloped societies or the major world powers, a sociological analysis would immediately reveal that their institutions have acquired two faces: one turned inward for the regulation of social life, and one oriented toward inter-societal relations. Certain aspects of the inter-societal environment have been "internalized," so to speak, into individual social structures. The state of ignorance of sociology with regard to such an obvious reality reminds one of the condition of individual psychology before social psychology emerged.

How far back in the evolution of culture must one go to find societies existing in isolation from one another, as strangers in a "state of nature"? At what point can one establish that societies exist in international environments which may themselves be treated as systems, i.e. as wholes which influence relations among interdependent parts? What kind of impact do such systems have on their participant units? Are international systems a product of social change, or are they among the prime causes of it?

Obviously, these questions cannot be adequately answered unless one has substantial knowledge of both social change and international relations. But lack of satisfactory knowledge is not really "ignorance," as was somewhat impulsively stated above.

Anyone acquainted with the history of social theory can point to a more or less extensive reference to inter-societal relations. As early as the 14th century, Ibn Khaldun of Tunisia, who certainly did not know he was a sociologist, had constructed a theory of social change based on international relations between nomadic and sedentary societies, using "solidarity" (Asabiyya) as his central category. Before and after Khaldun, many conflict theorists concerned with the origin and nature of the state had correlated international relations with social change in one way or another.[2] Yet perhaps only social Darwinists[3] attempted to systematize inter-societal relations (although only in terms of the evolutionary "struggle for survival"). In the 19th century more than one sociologist anticipated the need to regard external societies as performing internal functions in a given social system. Thus Pareto considered other societies as factors in the internal equilibrium of his social system. Even Durkheim, who concentrated on social integration, made the following, almost prophetic remark: ". . . the different nations of Europe are much less independent of one another, because, in certain respects, they are all parts of the same society, still incoherent, it is true, but becoming more and more self-conscious. What we call the equilibrium of Europe is a beginning of the organization of this society."[4] Later, in the preface to the second edition of *The Division of Labor in Society*, considering occupational corporations, he remarks: "We do not have to speak of international organizations which, in consequence of the international character of the market, would necessarily develop above this national organization. . . ."[5] Such excerpts are

[2] Polybius, Bodin, Ferguson, to mention but a few.
[3] Gumplowicz and Oppenheimer, among others.
[4] Emile Durkheim, *The Division of Labor in Society*, tr. by George Simpson (The Free Press, 1949), p. 121.
[5] *Ibid.*, p. 24.

CHAPTER 1

not the exception but the general rule in the writings of classical sociologists.

What about contemporary social science? Although there is some consciousness of the problem, and a certain amount of research has been done (especially on the transformation of traditional societies as dependent variables of industrial ones), there is little or no theoretical systematization. No comprehensive survey of relevant modern theories will be attempted here. However, without delving into the intricacies of those theories, it seems useful to further clarify the nature of the problem by some reference to modern social science.

Consider, for instance, the well-known observations of anthropologists on the inter-societal process of diffusion of cultural elements. Not only have most preliterate societies been exposed to its far-reaching influence, but certainly all "historical" societies as well. Ralph Linton illustrated the process in his vivid description of the daily activities of a "one-hundred per cent American."[6] In his estimation only about 10 per cent of contemporary American technology (let alone language, religion, political institutions, etc.) is due to local inventions. All the rest came by diffusion from other societies. It is doubtful whether any other technologically advanced society has a higher proportion of originality. Yet it is interesting to note that while diffusionist anthropologists would not venture beyond conceptions of historical contacts between unique cultures, the evolutionists, such as L. White and his followers, would use the data on diffusion to establish the reality of human culture at large, considered as a system evolving through definite stages.[7] This is not the place to delve into the paradoxes connected with the interpretation of diffusion. Even if one accepts the distinction between general and specific evolu-

[6] Ralph Linton, *The Study of Man* (Appleton, 1936), pp. 326-27.
[7] Leslie A. White, *The Evolution of Culture* (McGraw-Hill, 1959), pp. 17-18.

tion,[8] the incorporation of diffusion phenomena into a scheme of cultural evolution requires "intervening variables" between single cultures and culture in general. Suffice it to say, at this point, that investigation about durable inter-societal contacts in evolutionary or historical contexts is essential to the understanding of individual systems.

This, however, leads one to a not unrelated phenomenon. If cultural diffusion represents a way by which societies present *solutions of problems* to one another (e.g. a tool, a technique, an idea), there is also the parallel phenomenon of societies *introducing problems* into one another's systems. When viewed as interlocked political units impinging upon one another, any internal change in one system (economic, technological, military, ideological, etc.) which has a balance-changing significance for a coexisting system, might induce countervailing efforts in the latter. This indirect influence (as distinguished from direct interpenetration by cultural diffusion or forceful intrusion) represents the role played by coexisting societies in the structure of one another. Thus if they become participants in an inter-societal system, they must orient their institutions to one another. It is tempting to define such indirect but real influences as "transfunctions," since they reflect the consequences of one society's actions upon the structure of another. But here we reach an underdeveloped frontier of social theory and must proceed cautiously.

An immediate objection to the above trend of thinking might be directed at the apparent extension of social system concepts to the international level, since everyone knows that while the former is "integrated" the latter is not. Consider, for example, the following distinctions made by a political scientist: "If we look at the social sciences ... we see that these disciplines use as a model the image of the integrated community. ... In this society, social functions are differentiated and carried out in such a way that

[8] Marshall D. Sahlins and Elman R. Service, *Evolution and Culture* (University of Michigan Press, 1961), pp. 12-44.

the unity, harmony, or internal consistency of the society is achieved and maintained. Now, whatever else the nature of international relations may be, it is not an integrated system. It would be very dangerous in the long run to continue to work in a field with a model that does not fit."[9]

Certainly, there are fundamental differences between social systems and international systems, if only because their basic units differ. Yet from the perspective of historical sociology, or the evolution of culture, they both appear as evolving and interrelated forms of human organization with various levels of integration. What they have in common is that, unlike physical or organic systems, *their transformability of structure is a product of cumulative human action.* They both belong to the same class of phenomena, namely, the institutional, or culturological (as L. White would say), rather than the biological, psychological, or other. Furthermore, if it is the nature of integrated communities which explains such inter-societal relations as war, diplomacy, trade, alliances, protectorates, affiliations, and other disjunctive or conjunctive relations, then it might also be true that the nature of international relations explains significant aspects of integrated communities. They both have a historical character, i.e. they depend upon evolving conditions, and their functions change accordingly.

As for the concept of an "integrated social system," a closer look at modern sociology would reveal that it remains a problematic working hypothesis. There are increasing tendencies to open the conceptual system of sociology, to extend its boundaries, take it out of utopia, expose its incoherences, lags, and leads, and, last but not least, relate it to inter-societal relations. Consider, for example, the following observations:

> With reference to inter-system contacts, . . . the multiplication of agencies of communication serves to reduce

[9] Stanley Hoffmann (ed.) *Contemporary Theories in International Relations* (Prentice Hall, 1960), p. 3.

the isolation and thus the autonomy of societies, to increase the proportion and rate of changes from external sources, and thereby to increase "cultural" interdependence and even homogeneity.[10]

One particularly important source of exogenous change is a change originating in other social systems. For the politically organized society, the most important are other politically organized societies. *To consider change in this context, it is essential to treat the society of reference as a unit in a more inclusive social system.* Even when the system's level of integration is relatively low and chronic conflicts between its subunits continually threaten to break into war, some elements of more or less institutionalized order always govern their interrelations—otherwise, a concept like diplomacy would be meaningless. Of course, exogenous cultural borrowing and diffusion are mediated through interrelations among societies.[11] (Italics mine)

In other words, in seeking the factors of social change, sociologists arrive, among other things, at the problem of linkages between social systems. This might become a meeting ground with students of international relations who arrive at the problem of social change within societies which results from a changing international environment. Considered in isolation, however, the social system appears to some sociologists and political scientists as generating its own (endogenous) structural change. Let us further explore the logical interrelations between social change and international relations.

When sociologists engage in a search for determinants of

[10] Wilbert E. Moore, "A Reconsideration of Theories of Social Change," *American Sociological Review* (December 1960); see also, "Creation of a World Culture," *Confluence* (July 1955).

[11] Talcott Parsons, "An Outline of the Social System," in Parsons, et al. (eds.), *Theories of Society* (The Free Press, 1961), p. 71; see also Amitai Etzioni, "The Epigenesis of Political Communities at the International Level," *American Journal of Sociology*, LXVIII (1963), 407-21.

CHAPTER 1

social change they usually start with a logical elimination of extra-cultural factors, e.g. geographical, biological, etc. The argument goes like this: if some variable (culture) changes, and another variable (biological structure) is constant for the period in which change occurs, one cannot explain the changing variable by the unchanging. Whatever effects the constant might have produced, they were already present *before* the change in question took place. Therefore such constants are considered among the necessary but not the sufficient factors of social change. For example, in passing from feudalism to capitalism the climate, geography, and biological nature of England, or France, did not change. The logical conclusion is the explanation of social facts by antecedent and functional relations with other social facts, i.e. by identifying dependent and independent variables on the level of autonomous socio-cultural systems. The presupposition, of course, is the "organic" unity of society and its analytically impregnable "boundary maintenance." However, other societies, although external to any given society, are *not* environmental constants, but changing variables. It follows, therefore, that at least in the context of social change these variables form a unified framework.

Now, if one examines some leading theories of social change, it may be seen how the presupposition of organic unity can lead to fundamental distortions. Take, for example, Ogburn's hypothesis of "cultural lag." In essence it consists of three phases: an assumed integrated condition of the socio-cultural system; a developing lag between parts of culture, associated with maladjustments; and a process of mutual adaptation which tends to restore integration. The logic of the "lag" follows from a presupposition of a "functional lead." Thus, in Ogburn's terminology culture is divided into two mutually integrated sectors, material-utilitarian and nonmaterial-adaptive. The first (embodied in technology and its accumulative products) changes earlier and more rapidly than the instituted way of life, e.g. family patterns, legislation, education, government, etc. Various maladjustments result from the disproportionate development of parts which, serving as conditions of operation for one another, must belong together in a functioning organic unity, and the general course is for the nonmaterial to take an "adaptive" role. In other words, the functional lead of technology (independent variable) pushes the institutional order (dependent variable) into a condition of lag, and the process might be more appropriately termed "institutional lag."

This whole self-contained explanation is thrown out of order, however, if it can be shown that in some cases the lever which initiates a leading movement of technology stands *outside* the system, and if, in addition to causing internal imbalance, it modifies inter-systemic relationships. Thus the institutional lag might be, at least in part, relative to the inter-societal environment and to the adaptational response accordingly. It follows that the closure of such lags becomes also a function of adjustment *between* societies rather than merely within the organic unity of a given society. Consequently the process is neither entirely controlled by the properties of the social system nor is it resolved by the system alone. What, then, remains of the presupposed integration of social systems if one does not consider the effect of a combination of inter-systemic dynamics from without and polarities from within?

In what context, for example, can one understand the "atomic cultural lag" as formulated by Hornell Hart?[12] His two variables are the "killing area" and the "governing area"; the lag between these two variables is clearly in a field transcending the boundaries of a given social system, and in fact does not concern its inner balance. Political institutions are not shown there to be in disharmony with the leading acceleration of military technology if considered *within* the confines of the social system. Thus, no adaptation is necessary or possible here unless the social system is taken as a unit of an international system. Also, it means

[12] Hornell Hart, "Atomic Cultural Lag," *Sociology and Social Research*, Vol. 32 (1947-1948), 768-75, 845-55; see also, "Logistic Growths of Political Areas," *Social Forces* (1948).

that political institutions can be internally functional but externally disfunctional at the same time. Or, the other way around.

Likewise one can reconsider other theories of social change. Much before Ogburn's time, Karl Marx developed his "cultural-lag" theory between the "forces of production" (material culture) and the "relations of production" (adaptive culture); "maladjustment" in the form of the class struggle results in a revolution which reintegrates the social system. Here again the structural lag presupposes a functional lead and a semi-organic unity of the system. If, however, one ascertains from history that many economically based conflicts took place between tribes and nations rather than between classes; or that the rise and decline of classes (say, in the formation of feudal society) might be a consequence of the intrusion of foreign migratory ruling classes; or that social philosophies (such as Marxism itself) may travel between social systems by cultural diffusion— would this not tend to interfere with the "normal" dialectics of the social structure and produce developments which are unpredictable in the Marxian conceptual system? Does it account perhaps for his failure to foresee the coming of revolution in Russia (a participant in the inter-societal system of Europe)? Again, the Marxian system allows for the interpretation of capitalistic imperialism, but excludes the possibility of socialistic imperialism, even between socialistic societies. But this is not the place to elaborate on the subject. The point here is that, regardless of the institutional integration of social systems, no isolated and shiftless boundaries can be assumed, and their transformation cannot be understood apart from inter-societal relations.

Again, one can interpret Max Weber's theory of "rationalization" in terms of communal values lagging behind the development of impersonal bureaucracy. Problems of adjustment are created between these two aspects of social organization. In the Weberian scheme, as in the Marxian, the system must eventually integrate itself. Only the Weberian dialectic of transformation is idealistic, rather than materialistic, with respect to functional leads. Thus, the "Protestant ethic" gave direction to the "spirit of capitalism," which became the sufficient cause of "modern rational capitalism," a condition lacking in non-western societies. However oversimplified this account may be, it proves that the presupposition of organic unity and endogenous cultural change or resistance to change underlies the Weberian scheme, too. But it is not hard to show how international relations, historically examined, contributed tremendously to the very formation of "unique rationality" in Western Europe, and how in turn it brought about the grafting of the "spirit of modern capitalism" upon non-Protestant societies, both in Europe and in Asia. Inter-societal communication is certainly not a one-way process by which cultural achievements spread from a single historical spot. And thus the Weberian thesis on the development of "modern rational capitalism" conceived as a unique latent function of Protestantism appears somewhat ethnocentric.

Similarly, in Durkheim's conception of social change we have one of the clearest cases of organismic methodology stopping at the threshold of inter-societal relations. For the division of labor can lead from "mechanical solidarity" to "organic solidarity" only if the necessary integration of society is assumed. Thus, occupational differentiation, while increasing the interdependence of parts, must also transform the kind of solidarity which holds the system together. If "organic solidarity" is not perfectly realized, it is an expression of abnormality or anomie (normlessness) in Durkheim's terminology. The measure of anomie, then, is an index of institutional lag behind the functional lead of evolutionary structural differentiation. Could not the changing conditions, which induce the division of labor and the corresponding form of solidarity, be an expression of inter-societal trade or migration, or of the impingement of societies upon one another? Could not the political organization of power affect the organization of economic production? Now, we have already noticed Durkheim's anticipation of the social organization of European states "in consequence of the international character of the market." But this is not a structural differentiation of a preexisting organic whole; it is rather a formation of one from distinct and as-yet unintegrated units. Furthermore, if Durkheim were to explain occupational stratification within European societies, say under feudalism (or the Indian caste system), he could certainly not presuppose organic unity, and would have to consider inter-societal affiliation instead.

To sum up the discussion of this subject: whether one considers Ogburn's "cultural lag," or Marx's "relations-of-production lag," or Weber's "traditional lag," or Durkheim's "organic solidarity lag"—such phenomena as inter-societal diffusion, intrusion, and induced functions merge with the endogenous process of social change. All of these institutional lags presuppose a functional lead of one kind or another. But, as with the non-isolation of lags from inter-societal relations, so with the functional leads; the latter may also be new functions developing in response to inter-societal conditions.

At this point let us recapture the thread of our introductory questions. Is it reasonable or necessary to construct types of internationally related societies and examine, in this context, the problem of social change?

A Case Study with Experimental Value

The construction of types of historically evolved international systems requires empirical validation, and this is certainly not available in laboratories. Historical sociology, however, seems to be a suitable starting point. It can cautiously explore cases of experimental value without presupposing a general theory of social change or international relations. It might presuppose, however, the transformability of systems of human organization, their interaction and interdependence, and the cumulative process of institutionalization on the international level. At the present stage of knowledge in the field of historical sociology, it seems most desirable to select such case studies which promise experimental value without an overburdening complexity. It was with this purpose in mind that the present study took shape.

One of the questions that might shed light on the nature of the relationship between a given social system and its inter-societal environment is, what kind of change occurs when a social system is transplanted into a new and different political environment. This is not a frequent occurrence. The migration of a politically organized society with its entire institutional order is a circumstance of high experimental value. It is not the same as the immigration of groups or communities which may preserve cultural identity but cannot engage in international relations. If the circumstances of such a transplantation do not involve social changes which had already begun in the preceding inter-societal environment, then subsequent changes might be attributed to differences between the two inter-societal environments. Although this cannot be taken for granted, it is an opportunity for analysis which keeps internal social structure constant with respect to any other factor of change while varying the international factor.

Another question related to the transplantation of a political unit concerns the operation of traditional institutions. The latter, it is assumed, are adapted to function under a given set of conditions. To the extent that transplantation introduces new conditions, it automatically creates an institutional lag relative to the new international environment. This raises the interesting problem of what happens when adaptational tendencies with respect to the new inter-societal system are incongruent with the given social order, and consequently meet with built-in resistance. Does the mode of existence in various inter-societal systems shape the very nature of some pivotal social institutions? Does it determine their functions? And, if so, to what extent? How does internal stratification change, if at all, in response to forces operating on the inter-societal level?

Finally, a case of political transplantation raises such questions as, how does a given type of international system

CHAPTER 1

act and react to a newly introduced factor which constitutes an intrusive disturbance of balance? Other factors being equal, what changes might be attributed to *counter-adaptations* by all participants?

The case of the Latin Kingdom of Jerusalem in the Middle East seems to provide the above-mentioned combination of circumstances. The basic reasoning and expectations associated with this choice will follow presently, but the thesis as a whole will be unfolded through the entire study and concluded accordingly.

The meeting of the Crusaders' society with Islamic societies of the 12th century represents a transplantation of a political unit from one type of inter-societal environment (European feudalism) to a different one (the Middle Eastern frontier). The Crusaders entered the Middle East under political and military circumstances conducive to penetration but problematic with respect to long-range international relations. They eventually found themselves in an international system in which incompatible ideologies and a total threat to survival prevailed. This differed significantly from the European feudal system of institutionalized inter-princely skirmishes. Within the Crusaders' society, some adaptational innovations arose which played a central role in colonization and military defense, e.g. the religio-military orders. This movement combined knightly and monastic roles in collectivistic frontier communities. Its political functions were related to security and survival of their society. But the congruence of such innovations with the previously separated monastic and knightly ideals did not imply congruence with the entrenched stratification system and political institutions. Thus, the ensuing conflict between functional and culturally rooted *ideals*, and a disfunctional but institutionally supported *stratification system*, created a dilemma between social change and collapse of the social system.

Finally, the reaction of the fragmented Islamic states gave rise to ambitious empire builders and charismatic leadership. With the ensuing religious, cultural, and political renascence, local particularisms were welded together into the unified antagonistic solidarity of a Moslem empire. This powerful combination of military solidarity and a sacred ideology brought about the well-known culmination of the drama.

The case in question, then, viewed through the perspective of historical sociology, may be expected to yield the following:

1) A systematic observation of tendencies to social change resulting from transplantation of a politically organized society from one international system to another. The experimental value of this observation, however, is not limited to transplantation. For a society does not have to migrate in order to find itself, in time, operating in a definitely changed international system.

2) An exploration of the idea that societies interlocked in a prolonged conflict tend to affect one another's social organization in a process of response to developing needs implicated in the inter-societal system. When such a process occurs, it is reasonable to assume that various groups adapt first by institutionally known ways, and eventually tend to transform the functions of traditional roles to meet the exigencies of international survival.

3) A testing of the hypothesis that political collapse of a social system may be due to structural resistance to change, i.e. to institutional default with respect to changing conditions of international existence. In such cases a society detaches itself more and more from an impinging and unavoidable reality. Consequently, its actions become less and less effective, relative to the progressing discrepancy between new needs and culturally established functions.

4) An interpretation of the patterns exemplified by the Latin Kingdom of Jerusalem and its surrounding Islamic societies, considered as participants in a historically evolved international system.

Peoples' histories are not cut out for experimental purposes, even if observers may detect a certain logic in their development. The writer of historical sociology may be in-

CHAPTER 1

duced by the principle of relevance to conveniently arrange selected facts into a preconceived pattern, while ignoring non-confirming facts. If he attempts to avoid this distortion, a tension arises between his need to organize his material according to analytical categories and his duty to furnish the reader with a sufficiently broad description. In order to minimize this tension, it seems desirable to separate the analytical function from the descriptive one. The unfolding of historical events must not be blurred by efforts to establish theoretical significance, and vice versa. This simply means a consecutive arrangement of descriptive and analytical sections. Each historical section should be understood as a first approximation to the understanding of policies and actions, not as a presentation of "confirming evidence." The analysis following it will constitute an examination of "salient detail" considered in a sociological context. This may require the use of additional relevant materials, not necessarily mentioned in the descriptive section, in order to typify and illuminate the general. With these two distinct focuses, it is hoped that historical description will not appear subordinate in function to sociological analysis. And the latter, instead of presuming the ability to explain everything, will only attempt to render motives, actions, and events more intelligible by revealing the degree of their social determination.

In conformity to the historical unfolding of events it seems suitable to divide the material into the following phases:

1) The phase of transplantation from Europe to the Middle East and interlockage in a new international environment, including the initial military expansion and the political and economic consolidation achieved under Godfrey, Baldwin I, and Baldwin II (1099-1131).

2) The core of the Kingdom's history, consisting of precarious accommodations within the international system, including the critical turning points in the balance of power, with a gradually unifying Islam, roughly corre-

sponding to the kingships of Fulk, Baldwin III, and Amalric (1131-1174).

3) The period of culminating Moslem solidarity in Salah-ad-Din's empire vs. Latin demoralization, isolation, and collapse under the reigns of Baldwin IV, Baldwin V, and Gui de Lusignian (1174-1187).

Each of the above periods will serve as a point of departure for the immediately following chapter of sociological analysis. The latter will have to deviate somewhat from these historical compartments in order to point out the direction in which things were moving and their interrelationships.

Finally, the reader acquainted with the history of the Crusades may wonder about the reason for excluding the "Second Kingdom" of Acre (1191-1291) from consideration in the above framework. Although the European armies of the Third Crusade succeeded in reestablishing a Latin principality with a much reduced territory, they did not change the trend of social stagnation and political decline. At any rate, the later historical circumstances of the Kingdom of Acre involve remote and irrelevant factors that tend to break down the continuity of problems associated with the Kingdom of Jerusalem. This point will become clearer toward the end of my study.

Historical Interlockage

The Meeting of Normans and Saljuqs in the Middle East

Political uniformity was never a sustained feature of the eastern coast of the Mediterranean. Depending on the perspective of the observer, it may be viewed either as a crossroads of passing empires or as an inter-societal frontier consisting of local nationalities and foreign intruders. For one living on this frontier, existence always seemed connected with the necessity of reckoning with remote and overwhelming powers.

Even before the coming of the crusaders, three cumulative stages of international conflicts impinging upon this area may be distinguished. There was an ancient era, involving mainly a dual rivalry of intruding empires from the south and the northeast (Egyptians, Hittites, Assyrians, Babylonians, Persians). This was followed by a shift to conflicting pressures of west vs. east in the Greco-Roman era. In the course of the Islamic era, a triple rivalry developed: Fatimid Cairo from the south, Abassid Bagdad from the northeast, and Byzantine Constantinople from the northwest. The Crusades marked the opening of a new era with a fourth western power added to the existing three. Not incongruent with the spirit of the time, there were also four different organized churches involved in the rivalry.

One salient characteristic of this fourth era is the meeting of Normans and Saljuqs in the Middle East at the close of the 11th century. The Norman warriors, who set foot on the eastern coast of the Mediterranean, were interested in Christianity in the same political way that their chief ad-

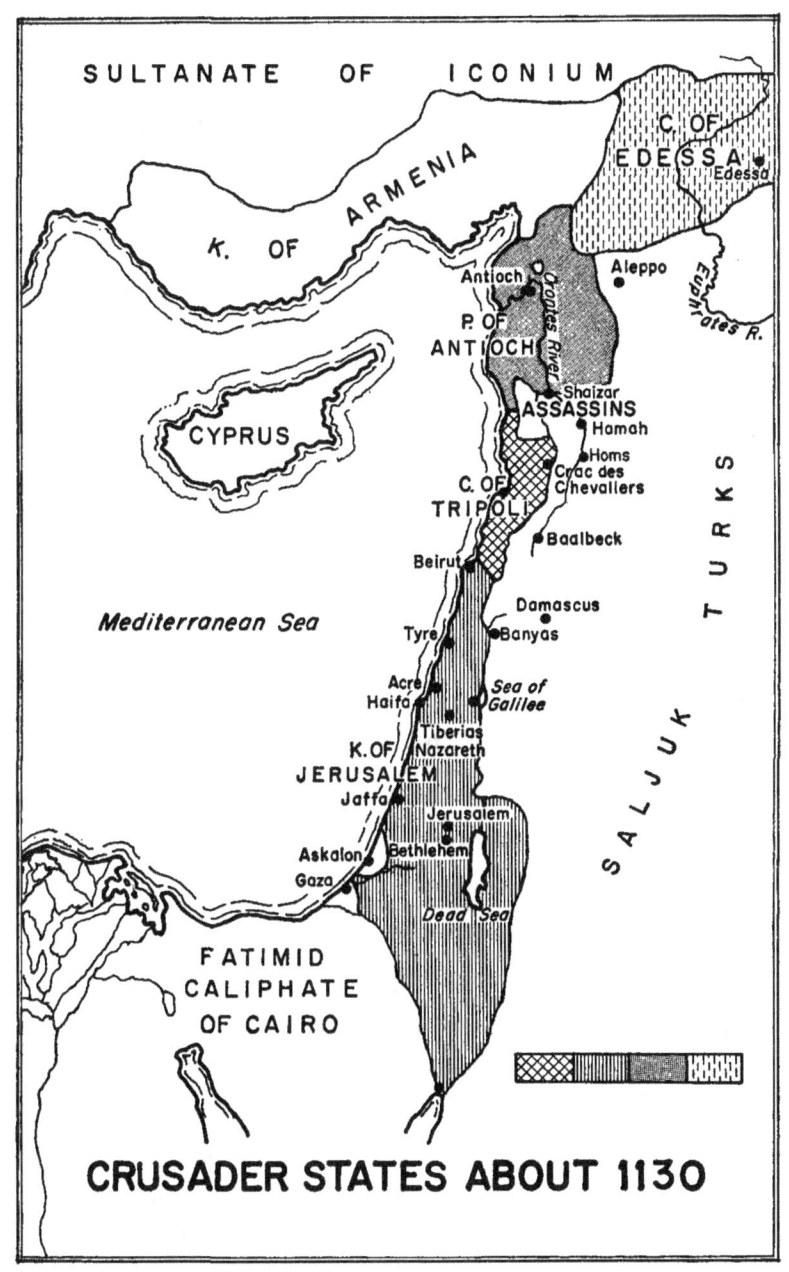

Map I: Crusader States about 1130
Adapted from Theodore Miller, in Sidney Painter,
A History of the Middle Ages (Knopf, 1954).

CHAPTER 2

versaries, the Saljuqs, were interested in Islam. Being both of recent barbarian origins, they kept moving into attractive centers of economic cultivation, utilizing their chief "means of subsistence," namely warfare. The parallel characteristics of these two power- and land-hungry migratory classes are striking indeed. Both Normans and Saljuqs had manifested a high degree of mobility. During one century the Normans had founded kingdoms in England, Italy, and Sicily, and the Saljuqs in Iran, Mesopotamia, Anatolia, and Syria. At the same time they were both serving as mercenaries in the imperial army of Byzantium, while their kinsmen were pushing against its frontiers from east and west with aims of conquest and inheritance. They offered themselves as protectors and servants of organized religion in their respective areas of expansion. But while Pope and Caliph viewed them as instruments of sacred purposes, they in turn employed their patronizers as ideology for secular pursuits. Having no roots anywhere, they assumed roles of migratory ruling classes with a capacity for political reform in vulnerable areas. Their struggle over "holy places" only reflected their main conflicting ambition to inherit the Byzantine empire and other inviting prizes around the Mediterranean.

However, neither Europe at large, with its plurality of rising forces, nor the vast Abassid realm, nor the weakened empires of Byzantium and Fatimid Egypt may be considered as merely participants in the new international system born with the crusaders' conquest of Jerusalem in the year 1099. All of these forces, peripheral as well as local, combined to produce or allow the establishment of the Latin Kingdom of Jerusalem. In this chapter we shall trace the various perspectives and activities of parties involved in the occurrence of this event. By delineating the historical and international conditions under which the Kingdom was formed and developed, we will prepare the ground for an analysis of its institutional adjustment or maladjustment to these conditions.

HISTORICAL INTERLOCKAGE

The Byzantine Perspective[1]

In Constantinople at the close of the 11th century there was no time for concern about "the holy land." The question was one of survival against waves of invasions from all directions. When Alexius Comnenus came to power in 1081 he faced the following problems:

1) How to check the Saljuqs from the east who had already crushed the imperial army at Manzikert (1071) and were establishing principalities all over Asia Minor. There was the Sultanate of Rum reaching up to Nicaea near the sea of Marmora and Constantinople. There was another Turkish principality quite secure in the east of Asia Minor, the Danishmends. And there was a Turkish "pirate," Tzachas, a former mercenary educated in Constantinople, who now had a fleet and territory on the southwestern coast of Asia Minor with Smirna as his capital. Tzachas had designs on the very throne of Byzantium, which he expressed not only by calling himself "basileus," but by making actual military alliances with other potential conquerors, who came very close to their aim. Thus, the eastern half of the empire was being partly Islamized and resettled by Turcoman tribes, partly plundered and devastated, with a mass relocation of Christians and a vast transfer of lands into Turkish control. Alexius' personal riches in land lay in Anatolia.

2) How to check the advance of the Normans from the west, who had already driven Byzantium out of southern Italy, and were presently invading it through the Adriatic

[1] The facts as well as some elements of interpretation in this section, are drawn mainly from the following secondary sources: A. A. Vasiliev, *History of the Byzantine Empire*, Vol. II (University of Wisconsin Press, 1961); J. M. Hussey, *The Byzantine World* (Harper Torchbooks, 1961); Steven Runciman, *A History of the Crusades*, Vol. I (Cambridge University Press, 1957); Peter Charanis, "The Byzantine Empire in the Eleventh Century," in M. Setton and M. W. Baldwin (eds.), *A History of the Crusades*, Vol. I (University of Pennsylvania Press, 1958); François L. Ganshof, *Le Moyen Age*, in Pierre Renouvin (ed.), *Histoire Des Relations Internationales*, Vol. I (Paris, 1953).

CHAPTER 2

coast with the blessing of Pope Gregory VII. The son of the leader of this campaign, Bohemond (later one of the major commanders of the First Crusade), was at the beginning of a get-Constantinople career that would have put him on equal footing with his brother Roger, who engaged successfully in a get-Sicily career. Alexius also remembered a significant episode with a certain Norman mercenary, Roussel, who had led a rebellion of 3,000 Normans within the empire's territory in the midst of the struggles with the Turks.

3) How to repel the increasingly threatening assaults of the Pechenegs and Uzes from the northwest in the Balkans. These were other Turks who had become conscious of their affinity with the Saljuqs through international contacts on Byzantine territory. They had defeated the imperial army before Alexius's accession, and had wrested various concessions from it. In the first ten years of Alexius' rule, however, they came very close to the actual conquest of Constantinople.

4) Further complications in both foreign and internal policy involved such issues as the break in relations between the Greek and Roman Catholic Churches; constant political plotting against the throne by two competing parties, the landed military aristocracy of the empire (from whom Alexius himself had gained leadership) and the urban bureaucracy of imperial management; control of recurrent threats by the restless Hungarian bands; and, last but not least, control of the multi-national mercenary army of the empire, itself a political system in a precarious balance. The semi-feudal social organization of the Byzantine empire had reached a point at which reliance upon mercenaries became preponderant over recruiting from a free peasantry.

Under the pressure of such emergencies, the only effective initiative Alexius could take was diplomacy. Through wide-ranging diplomatic efforts, he managed to play one enemy against another, or to involve enemies of his enemies in his cause, if not by the principle of "divide and rule," at least through the "divide and save your skin" method. Thus, he succeeded in getting the Sultan of Nicaea, Kilij Arslan, to kill his rival, Tzachas of Smirna; he got decisive maritime aid from Venice against the Norman invasion (at the price of commercial concessions), and could have received help from his friend Henri IV if the latter had not been too entangled in his conflict with the Pope; he mobilized the Cumans (barbarians from Russia) to destroy the Pechenegs just before the latter were about to crush his empire. Only after 1092, when the Turkish emirs of Asia Minor seemed embroiled in internal strife (see below, pp. 32-33), when the Normans had been repelled at least temporarily, and the Pechenegs crushed, did Alexius start to think in terms of supplementing diplomacy with military initiative. For that he needed more mercenaries and, if possible, some political partners. Against this background he wrote to Pope Urban II for help in recruiting Christian military units against the "enemies of Christianity" in Asia Minor and the Holy Land. This idea was not entirely novel in Constantinople; there had been some precursory contacts on the matter, upon which we need not dwell here.

Therefore, nothing could look more encouraging to Alexius and his counselors than the sight of Norman knights, although somewhat frightening in their numbers, crossing the Bosphoros toward bloody engagements with another enemy of Byzantium, the Saljuqs of Asia Minor. The Normans, of course, were only part of a much larger Christian expedition, already known as a Crusade to the Holy Land, which to Alexius meant a chance to revive Byzantine control all the way up to Syria, with crusading principalities incorporated into the empire and serving as buffer units on the frontier with Islam.

From the perspective of Constantinople, then, the year 1099 marked a definite improvement over the circumstances of only seven years before. Instead of worrying about the capital falling into the hands of Pechenegs or Normans, Alexius now faced such new problems as controlling the recaptured areas in Asia Minor and attaching Armenian and crusaders' principalities to the imperial function of buffer states. On the whole, the self-image of Byzantium tended to blend positively with the image imputed to the Kingdom of Jerusalem. Although not entirely free of new anxieties, this new situation meant to Byzantium some relief from the serious threats of the past, tangible accomplishments in the present, and some promising prospects for the future. If it had been up to Constantinople only, good diplomatic relations would have been established with Jerusalem with far-reaching results for the future of both.

The Perspective of the Italian Maritime Cities (Genoa, Pisa, Venice)[2]

Far from being united among themselves, these rising powers had a common enthusiasm for the coast of the Holy Land, be it in the name of a Crusade or any other "cause." Before the 11th century they were part of a frontier in defense against Moslem expansions, hardly capable of holding onto their commercial positions, and adjusting to the realities of raids and plunderings on their own territory. Now, however, the historical tide was well in reverse. With stretched maritime muscles and incipient commercial exploits in the western Mediterranean they were now completing an almost century-old offensive against the weakening Moslem positions. Genoa and Pisa conquered nearby islands, established new and prospering trading posts, and in 1087 were able to mobilize 400 ships in a punitive capture of the rich commercial port of North Africa, al Mahdia. Meanwhile, Venice had secured a commercial route between Alexandria, Northern Syria, and Constantinople, reaching north into the Black Sea and west into Europe. Thus she was vitally interested in any change of power

[2] This concise section is based on the sources mentioned in n. 1, above, and on A. R. Lewis, *Naval Power and Trade in the Mediterranean (500-1100)* (Princeton University Press, 1951); and Hilmar C. Krueger, "The Italian Cities and the Arabs Before 1095," in Setton and Baldwin, *A History of the Crusades*, Vol. I.

positions in the Mediterranean. She could hardly ignore the new developments.

With the western and central parts of the Mediterranean under their control, and with the Norman conquest of Sicily completed, nothing could be more attractive than trading posts in the east. Had the organizers of the First Crusade not been so ignorant about communication conditions, they could have saved more than half of their marching manpower by availing themselves of safe transportation on Italian ships. Even so, Genoa, Pisa, and Venice did not fail to show up in Antioch, Jaffa, Haifa, and Acre. They not only viewed the establishment of the Kingdom of Jerusalem favorably, but actively joined in the offensive. In fact, their intervention was decisive to the very success of the First Crusade. They came to stay, in a way, and were adequately rewarded by special concessions in the ports they helped to capture (see below, pp. 36-39).

If there was no great affection between Franks and Italians, there was certainly an air of mutual instrumentality. From the shores of Genoa, Pisa, and Venice, the Kingdom of Jerusalem appeared as the right thing at the right time and in a desirable location. Their ears were tuned, however, not so much to the ring of church bells from the Holy Sepulchre as to the ring of camel caravans from Damascus. Rome was back in Palestine, this time not with legionnaires, but with its own commercial colonizers, under the auspices of former barbarians, and with the spiritual guidance of a not-quite-foreign religion.

The Perspective of the Roman Catholic Church[3]

The papacy of the 11th century was an international institution with two major faces. It was the head of a west-

[3] This section is based on the sources mentioned in n. 1 and: Jean Richard, *Le Royaume Latin de Jérusalem* (Presses Universitaires de France, 1953); Joshua Prawer, *A History of the Latin Kingdom of Jerusalem*, Vol. I (The Bialik Institute, 1963); Fredric Duncalf, "The Councils of Piacenza and Clermont," in Setton and Baldwin, *A History of the Crusades*, Vol. I.

CHAPTER 2

ern Christian "City of God" with spiritual, educational, and judicial functions cutting across ethnic and political boundaries. At the same time, it constituted an autonomous political unit, manipulating military means, controlling territories, directly and indirectly, engaging in balance-of-power relations, and peculiarly involved in economic and social processes. In other words, it was a real, though not ordinary, "City of Man."

This is not the place for a comprehensive analysis of the institution, but it is important to understand that the idea of a Crusade reflected the theocratic nature of the medieval Catholic Church. Thus the appointment of Bishop Adhemar as overlord of the lay feudal armies bent on establishing a feudal theocracy in Jerusalem, or the expedition of a Pisan fleet headed by another bishop, Daimbert, as well as the later assumption of direct control over the religio-military orders, all of these acts reflected theocratic interests. One cannot fully appreciate the significance of such acts without a knowledge of the wider strategies and aspirations of the Church.

It is customary among historians to trace the political aspects of the Church to the Cluniac Movement of the 10th century, with its organizational and ideological reforms. But actually the seeds of politization were planted long before, in the mutual adaptation of nobility and clergy as a composite and interdependent ruling caste. In the 11th century Gregory VII was attempting to change the established feudal balance between these two components of the elite. He aspired to consolidate supreme authority in his own hands, so as to subordinate the emperor and use him as a central agency of Christian control. Gregory's policies relied for their success on diplomacy backed by manipulation of military powers; his position was similar in principle to that of the Byzantine emperor in his time of stress. Thus, he resisted Henry IV in the investiture controversy by the forces of rebellious princes in Germany; he made alliances with the Normans in Italy for mutual support of expansionistic designs; he opposed the non-cooperation of Philip I in

France by aligning with his political rivals; and he negotiated with Byzantium a union of the churches, while at times considering military aid to her and at times supporting an invasion of her territory. It was only natural for him to conceive the idea of a Crusade with himself as commander in the framework of extensive imperial dreams.

His disciple, Urban II, who ascended the pontifical chair in 1088, was a Frenchman with political ties in southern France. He inherited a number of political complications and crises, including a puppet anti-Pope in Rome, but still had sufficient resources to embark on a more realistic international policy. He restored diplomatic relations with Alexius in 1089, and established good relations with Conrad, the heir to the German throne, to the extent of having him rebel against his father. There were wealthy monasteries everywhere to recognize his authority, and a great number of counts, lords, and bishops who would lend him their support. Urban definitely carried on the Gregorian outlook, and when he received a call for help from Alexius in 1095, he had only to reconstruct the Gregorian dream of a Crusade. Well acquainted with the political disorders in central and northern France as a result of a surplus of warriors without land, and with the responsiveness of southern French lords to the opening of a second front with Islam, he decided to initiate a movement on a grand scale. His design surpassed the particular bid of Byzantium. He probably had in mind such "by-products" as the annexation of the eastern church, a diversion of Normans away from central Italy, a utilization of maritime forces from Pisa and Genoa under papal patronage, the Peace and Truce of God in France, and a reinvigorated voice in general European affairs.

The Council of Piacenza and its culmination in the sermon of Clermont on November 27, 1095, which resulted in the initiation of a massive Crusade, were evidently not matters of spontaneous inspiration. Even though the dimensions of the First Crusade were unanticipated, no other political unit in Europe at the time could have the perspective and authority required for the initiation of a movement on such an international scale. From the viewpoint of the Church, the crusaders indeed deserved all the absolutions and other concessions conferred upon them. Yet some humble and underprivileged young sons, such as a Baldwin and a Tancred, or some anonymous Italian merchants, must have been aware from the outset that earthy opportunities, much less grandiose but still desirable, lay ahead of them.

Individual motives aside, the Pope and his counselors did initiate a new turn to the existing multi-dimensional expansion of the European frontiers of which they themselves were a part. They knew about the progress of reconquest in Spain. They watched with mounting hopes the successes of their Norman "vassals" in Sicily, and the decisive victories of Italian fleets in the Mediterranean. They reacted positively to the Norman conquest of England. They were informed of forest clearing and settlement in eastern Europe across the Slavic frontier, and they took account of the steady Christianization of Hungarians, Slavs, and Scandinavians. Their Europe at the close of the 11th century was no longer a helpless prey to Vikings, Madiars, and Saracens.

How else could all these expanding potentials of a practically illiterate and quarrelsome population be channeled (by a church!) except in a Holy War? If the Peace of God and the Truce of God could not work, the War of God would. The center of gravity for the Church still remained in Europe, but with the initiation of the First Crusade its universal role took on new dimensions, with far-reaching political implications.

The Saljuqid and Syrian Perspectives[4]

Nominally a theocratic empire, with the forms and insignia of Harun al-Rashid, the Abassid Caliphate of Bag-

[4] This section is based on the sources mentioned in n. 1 and: W. B. Stevenson, *The Crusaders in the East* (Cambridge University Press, 1907); Ibn al-Qalanisi, *The Damascus Chronicle of the Crusades* (tr. and introduced by H.A.R. Gibb) (Luzel & Co., 1932); Claude Cahen,

dad in the 11th century was in an authentic "Babylonian Exile." The process of institutional decline and political disintegration had started much earlier, but our concern here is with developments immediately preceding the appearance of crusading armies in Syria. Had these inspired invaders come to Syria five years earlier, while there was still an empire headed by the Saljuq Sultan, Malik-Shah, with his brothers, sons, uncles, and cousins still cooperating, and Turcoman horsemen still organized under one central authority, there is no doubt that they would have been quickly destroyed. As it was, any army that had entered Syria after 1092, i.e. after the death of Malik-Shah and the ensuing civil wars, would have made a lucky strike.

The political story in essence began about forty years earlier, when a recently Islamized Turkish chief, Tugril-Beg, entered Bagdad with his army by invitation of a powerless caliph, and received a newly instituted title, Sultan. Two or perhaps three socio-cultural strata were linked through this symbolic act: Turkish barbarians of various tribal traditions; urban Iranian, Mesopotamian, and Syrian Moslems; and Arab tribes of various localities in the Middle East. The Turkish warriors proceeded to build a semi-feudal state, establishing a new elite of iqtah- (fief) holders with mounted armies at the service of a tribal leadership, while the civilized Moslems, under the leadership of the wazir, Nizam-al-Mulk, organized judicial, financial, and administrative services and a network of educational institutions. On the regional-local level, the Turks tolerated, in fact, relied upon tribal or municipal home rule. This Saljuqid dynasty, despite several glorifying and rewarding military successes, lasted only three generations as a unified body. Their climax came in the tremendous expansion of Alp-Arslan (who had broken the backbone of the Byzantine army at Manzikert in 1071); then came an apparent

---

"The Turkish Invasion: The Selchükids" in Setton and Baldwin, *A History of the Crusades*, Vol. I; Claude Cahen, *La Syrie du Nord à l'Epoque des Croisades* (Librairie Orientaliste Paul Geuthner, 1940).

CHAPTER 2

consolidation under Malik-Shah, followed by its fragmentation after his death. A full explanation for this is irrelevant in this context. It is important only to mention the institution of "atabegate" in the Saljuqid system. An atabeg was an elderly general entrusted with guarding and serving a young enfiefed prince of the royal family. He could marry the mother of his trustee and give him their daughter to cement the ties. Or he could kill him and inherit his principality without necessarily disrupting the feudal alignment with superiors. Or he could break with him if military circumstances so enabled and try to get hold of another power position elsewhere. The whole Saljuqid domain was soon proliferated into a series of semi-independent power positions. The traditional solidarity was drowned in political rivalry and material prosperity. Waves of nomadic kinsmen infiltrated throughout the land, serving as a reservoir of military recruiting for various power rivalries.

When Malik-Shah died in 1092, a catastrophic period of civil wars began. As one historian puts it: "Hence there developed quarrels among the sons of Malik-Shah and between them and his brothers, their uncles being enemies of the family of Nizam-al-Mulk. This situation resulted in a partition of the empire, devastation, administrative disorder, and universal usurpation. For what had begun in 1092 got worse with every later change of ruler. Each prince in an effort to secure allies disposed of resources and territories and thus weakened himself by that much."[5]

Syria was at the time the domain of Tutush, a brother of Malik-Shah who disputed the succession to the Sultanate with Barkyaruk, the Sultan's son. There were battles in Iran and Syria, and finally in 1095 Tutush was defeated and killed near Teheran. He left behind him two sons with their atabegs in Aleppo and Damascus; they in turn broke into a familial war. According to one historian, "It was this battle [in Iran] which decided the fate of the First Crusade. Had the crusaders been met with the combined resources of the

[5] Claude Cahen, "The Turkish Invasion," in Setton and Baldwin.

unitary kingdom built up by Tutush, history would certainly have been rewritten; as it was, his hard-won Syrian possessions were again disintegrated by the rivalries of his sons Rudwan and Duqaq and the jealousy and self-seeking of his former generals."[6]

When the crusaders started on their way, then, Syria was fighting a civil war, with a number of Turkish generals and Turcoman emirs switching sides. The war continued well into 1097, when they received news about the arrival of Frankish armies in northern Syria.

Strangely enough, the alliances broke down, with each partner hurrying to his own city. The strongest, Yagi-Siyan, of Antioch, was left alone to defend his land against a siege which lasted for almost a year. Meanwhile, the Arab cities on the coast and in the interior of Syria and Palestine were hardly prepared to take any initiative beyond local resistance. These were fragmentary political units, partly aligned with Egypt and partly under Saljuqid suzerainty. The invasion of armies from the Byzantine direction was not unfamiliar to them; in fact, in a sense it helped to balance the pressures of Saljuqid imperialism with which they were still preoccupied.

The perspectives? They corresponded in number and character to the bewildered self- and imputational images of the area. But Islamic solidarity was latent and ominous.

The Egyptian Fatimid Perspective[7]

Although it was an eccentric Fatimid caliph, al-Hakim, who had destroyed the Holy Sepulchre in 1009, and even though it was from a short-lived Egyptian government that the crusaders took Jerusalem in 1099, neither religious fanaticism nor military vigor were characteristic of Egypt at the turn of the century. Decline in spite of administrative

[6] H.A.R. Gibb, *Introduction to The Damascus Chronicle of the Crusades* by al-Qalanisi, p. 21.

[7] This section is based on the sources mentioned in nn. 1-4, above, and R. Grousset, *Histoire des Croisades et du Royaume Franc de Jérusalem*, 3 vols. (Paris, 1934-1936).

CHAPTER 2

reforms was the trend. Early historical ambitions to establish a Shiite empire from Cairo to Bagdad had long since vanished. A gradual retreat from all of Syria except the coastal cities took place during the 11th century. This process was a combined result of former Byzantine pressure, frequent rebellions of Arab tribes, and Saljuqid expansion after 1075. Egypt too had some Turkish mercenaries. How could she avoid them if she was to combat the Abassid Turkish regiments? On the Egyptian soil the Turks were Shiites rather than Sunnites. Starting as slave-soldiers, they eventually aspired to political power, and were involved in a series of civil wars together with Berber and Sudanese troops. From 1062 to 1073 Egypt was drowned in confusion. A certain governor of Acre, Badr al-Jamali, and later his son, Al-Afdal, who were Armenian by descent and Sunnite by faith, came to Egypt on the invitation of a desperate caliph. They became wazirs and took over the leadership from the decaying caliphate. Badr al-Jamali, after suppressing military dissensions, instigated an "administrative revolution." Establishing himself as both a political and military head, he divided the country into estates whose income was assigned to army officers, thus giving the latter social security and stability. The commerical resources of Egypt allowed him to build a salaried administration, under his supervision, which organized all payments to and from the government. This integration of military and civic functions was a remarkable achievement, but was no substitute for the religious or national solidarity essential to the success of large kingdoms. It sufficed, however, to keep the internal mercenaries under control and the external enemies out—temporarily.

Badr al-Jamali's son, Al-Afdal, could not view the invasion of the crusaders with indifference, since they were Christians conquering Egyptian holdings in Palestine; but neither could he overlook the fact that they were getting between him and the Saljuqs of the north. His outlook was ambivalent and hesitant, as may be inferred from his early negotiations with them and his essentially defensive campaigns against them. Al-Afdal could not be too disturbed by the loss of Syrian seaports, since Egyptian commercial prosperity depended mainly on the Red Sea trade linking the Far East with Constantinople via Alexandria and Damietta. Syria did have its local economic significance, but much more profitable trade was being distracted from the turbulent Abassid-Byzantine frontiers. Egyptian and Venetian merchants benefited most from this change, while Greeks and Syrians suffered.

To Egyptians, as to most Syrians, Moslem as well as Christian, the crusaders appeared at first as the equivalent of a historically familiar Byzantine penetration. It was not inconceivable for them to renew the traditional balance-of-power strategies of the area. But, were the Frankish lords at all aware of the serious choice between alliance with Byzantium or alliance with Egypt? Their first generation was certainly not.

The Establishment of Crusaders' Principalities[8]

The loose federation of crusading forces was an expedition of imperial dimensions without imperial organization. True, the Church conferred upon them a unifying sacred mission and invested its own representative, Bishop Adhemar, with supreme legitimate authority over the entire expedition. But it was clear from the outset that this formal overlordship of the Church did not infringe upon the actual authority of the princes over their feudally bound armies. The latter remained autonomous political units, acting as an alliance and cooperating voluntarily by consent and by military expediency. Moreover, the lords and their men were not merely disinterested "pilgrims" with otherworldly motives. They had secular aims in mind, and the fact that the land they were going to conquer was "holy" did not diminish its value as property. Politically speaking,

[8] This section is based on the sources mentioned in nn. 1-4, 7, and Dana C. Munro, *The Kingdom of the Crusaders* (Appleton, 1935); William of Tyre, *History of Deeds Done Beyond the Sea* (tr. by Babcock and Krey) (Columbia University Press, 1943).

CHAPTER 2

the partnership of such incompatible leaders as Raymond of Toulouse, Bohemond and Tancred of Norman Italy, Godfrey and Baldwin of Bouillon, the two Roberts of Normandy and Flanders, was inherently tentative, to say the least. They fought successful battles against the Saljuqs of Anatolia, persisting with a unified determination only up to the border of Syria. Thereupon all political cards emerged from under the table, and a struggle over inheritances began. Their spiritual leader, Adhemar, died during the siege of Antioch, and there was no recognized Joshua to lead them into the Promised Land.

Thus, while the main camp was surrounding the walls of Antioch, Baldwin went across the Euphrates River to found a private principality among native Armenian fellow Christians in the city of Edessa. Bohemond with his body of Norman knights, seeing in Antioch an attractive bird-in-the-hand, lost his desire to reach far-away Jerusalem. Antioch had rich lands, a river, a nearby port, and, most significantly, it was close to the Byzantine frontier. Even Raymond, whose Christian piety was notorious, could not resist earthly temptations which conflicted with crusading commitments. Unable to challenge Bohemond with respect to Antioch, he turned south to Tripoli as an acceptable compensation for his Provencals. In this way the foundations of three northern principalities (Edessa, Antioch, and Tripoli) were laid before the Holy Land was even in sight.

The spirit of the First Crusade, however, was too strong to be divided by such deviant feudal acquisitiveness. There was sufficient idealism in the rank and file and rising expectations among secondary leaders to create pressure for carrying the march on towards Jerusalem. For reasons indicated above, the way to Jerusalem was clear of any major armies except for the fortified ports along the coast, which were bypassed. However, the choice of the coastal road indicated some dependence upon Italian fleets. Jaffa was taken with the help of a Pizan fleet. The fleet of Genoa which had already contributed to the conquest of Antioch was now on its way to aid in the siege of Jerusalem. A large

Venetian fleet was being prepared for the following year's campaigns. Thus, except for the major confrontations with the Saljuqs of Asia Minor, and a decisive engagement near Antioch, there were no serious battles to fight on the way to Jerusalem. The city was helplessly waiting for a brief siege, a breakthrough, and a massacre of practically all non-Christians.

Presently, a second round of jealous intrigues and power struggles developed among the crusading princes. Godfrey of Bouillon was elected to leadership as a compromise between the higher ranking lords. He was given the ambiguous title, "Defender of the Holy Church," but had no intention of yielding actual power to the patriarch except as a religious authority. It was not long before old political rivalries were renewed in the crusading camp. This was manifested at the siege of Askalon, an important port which served as an Egyptian base. The Askalonians intended to surrender to Raymond of Toulouse because they considered him trustworthy after his exceptionally moderate conduct in Jerusalem. This opportunity was sabotaged by Godfrey himself, and Askalon successfully renewed its resistance. Consequently, the armies of Normandy and Flanders declared their crusading mission ended and started their return to Europe. Raymond and his Provencals turned northward to their Syrian domain, while Tancred the Norman began an expansion into Galilee with clear plans for independence. The remaining forces were still divided on the unavoidable power issue between Godfrey and the patriarch, who still believed that Jerusalem was not to become a regular feudal kingdom. The ensuing civil war was further complicated by the sudden and untimely death of Godfrey. It could have ended with an open Franko-Norman clash, if it had not been for Bohemond's falling into Turkish captivity, and for Baldwin of Edessa (Godfrey's brother), who came down to Jerusalem to seize power at the invitation of his brother's vassals. Tancred was compelled to replace Bohemond in Antioch, and the way was cleared for Baldwin's succession to Godfrey's position.

CHAPTER 2

From a landless younger son, who had once aspired to an ecclesiastic career, to the ruler of Jerusalem was not an easy climb without initiative, imagination, and bravery. All of these were much-needed qualities in the new principality.

Precarious Interlockage of the Kingdom of Jerusalem

Baldwin I (1100-1118) is rightly recognized as the founder of a solid kingdom stretching from Ailat on the Red Sea to Beirut in the north. He blocked ecclesiastical aspirations to a theocratic overlordship by putting the ambitious Patriarch Daimbert in a traditional place and by establishing a normal feudal monarchy. With very small military means he resisted the yearly Egyptian attempts to destroy the Kingdom in its infancy, and he conquered all the coastal towns between Jaffa and Beirut except for Tyre. He welded together baronies and fiefs and guaranteed Frankish control over the entire conquered territory by subordinating the productive local population. He promoted the settlement of merchants and craftsmen in the devastated towns. It was Baldwin I who built the first fortresses and castles, chartered the early extra-feudal organizations, and was able to support and lead the sister principalities in northern Syria. All this, however, is just one side of the coin. The other side consists of elements which are perhaps more important for understanding the precarious future of the Latin Kingdom of Jerusalem.

Baldwin's successes contained two significant aspects of weakness. The first had to do with the fact that the real conquerors of the coastal towns were the fleets of Genoa, Piza, and Venice. The second concerned latent dangers from the Saljuqid-Byzantine frontier in northern Syria in which the Normans and Franks became unwittingly entangled.

Italian intervention enabled the 500 knights who remained in the Kingdom of Jerusalem with their 2,000-3,000 foot soldiers to exploit their great opportunity. The military and political vulnerability of Syria at the outset of the First Crusade has been described above. It was not until 1110 that a strong army from Mesopotamia appeared in Syria (under Maudud of Mosul), raising the banner of Jihad (Holy War) in the name of the caliph and the Saljuqid sultan. It was not an accident that this coincided with the end of Frankish expansion (except for Tyre, which was conquered with the aid of the large Venetian navy in 1124). This clearly indicates Jerusalem's desperate need, from the outset, of unconventional countervailing forces against threats to its very existence from the Moslem periphery.

The initial dependence of the Kingdom on Italian naval support was reflected in the great commercial concessions granted to them in return for military aid. Agreements were made mainly with Genoa and Venice whereby a certain quarter of each conquered town was granted to them, including a market, a church, and other institutions deemed necessary for the settlement of a new colony. Most significantly the Italians insisted upon and received exemptions from customs and duties along with some judicial autonomy, which opened the way for commercial colonization of the coastal towns. There is sufficient evidence that these concessions were granted not against the will of Jerusalem's policy makers, but rather as part of a positive plan to develop the resources of their kingdom. Thus, Baldwin also invited Christian natives from Transjordan to settle in Jerusalem, and even non-Christians were induced to engage in special crafts.[9] But the baronial class as a whole did not see in these commercial colonies more than limited advantages.

The second aspect of weakness may be referred to as the fatal entanglement in northern Syria. The divided goals of the First Crusade were reflected mainly in the detachment of Normans from Franks of central and northern France, and from Provencals. Thus, while one leader, Raymond of Toulouse, established good diplomatic relations with Byzantium and cooperated with their wish to return to northern

---

[9] See J. Prawer, "The Settlement of the Latins in Jerusalem," *Speculum*, Vol. XXVII (October 1952), 490-503, for a detailed analysis of early colonization in the Kingdom.

CHAPTER 2

Syria, the Normans Bohemond and Tancred rebuked early agreements with the Byzantines and engaged in a series of military campaigns against them. Antioch conducted a completely independent policy in the first decade of the crusaders' history. Bohemond had grand designs of his own, encompassing perhaps the control of all Syria and/or the Byzantine empire. Without going into much detail we can see from their movements what the Normans were after. They conquered the Cilician towns of Anatolia; they stimulated Armenian forces to reject Byzantine suzerainty; they attacked the Greeks who set foot on the Syrian coast together with the Provencals; earlier Tancred had conquered Galilee and made a bid for power in the Kingdom of Jerusalem. Frustrated by the Palestinian Franks, who were loyal to Baldwin, and attracted to the vacancy created in Antioch by the captivity of Bohemond (1100-1103), Tancred went there to engage in expansion in all directions, to the extent of cooperating with Moslem allies against the Franks of Edessa. When Bohemond returned, an ambitious Norman advance beyond the Euphrates took place. It could have led to Norman hegemony over all of northern Syria with Aleppo and Edessa swallowed thereby. Frustrated, however, by Saljuqid counteroffensives which drove the Normans back to the Orontes River near Antioch, Bohemond, returned to Europe to organize a whole new Crusade. Heralded there as a great crusader, he was able to coordinate a large expedition, which he led not to the Holy Land but to Byzantium. His attempt to invade the empire from the West failed (1107), as had the first Norman invasion by Robert Guiscard (Bohemond's father), mainly through maritime superiority on the Greek side. The subdued Bohemond agreed to relinquish Antioch to the Byzantines, but Tancred held the land with a strong Norman army. The Norman threat to Byzantium in northern Syria remained, while the possibility of European danger from the west cast a dark shadow on all future relations between the crusaders and Byzantium.

HISTORICAL INTERLOCKAGE

While the Byzantines were alienated from crusading interests in Syria, the Saljuqs of Mesopotamia were aroused to fear and alarm. Even the Armenians, relieved as they felt by the advent of the Crusades from both Greek and Saljuqid oppression, were not quite ready to substitute Norman or Frankish oppression for the former ones. The predominantly Armenian principality of Edessa with its surrounding towns found itself under new masters rather than united with Christian allies. Baldwin I, who had started his career in the east by conquering Edessa, now had a vassaldom there with a handful of Frankish knights led by Baldwin II, later his successor. Therefore, he took his Jerusalemite army there as often as he could to fight battles. His aim was to become a suzerain of all the Latin principalities in Syria, which after the conquest of Tripoli (1109) became three in number and quite hostile toward each other.

By that time the yearly campaigns of the unified Saljuqid forces of Maudud had started, and Baldwin was forced to rush into defensive battles throughout Syria. In 1113 Maudud invaded the Kingdom of Jerusalem itself, with prospects not less threatening than Salah-ad-Din's invasions seventy years later. The resources of the Franks in manpower and equipment diminished rapidly, but they had a respite after Maudud's assassination in Damascus. Then came the great victory of Roger (Tancred's successor in Antioch) over the Saljuqs near Danith in 1115. Only at this point was Baldwin free to start organizing the Kingdom of Jerusalem. This was the year in which he was able to concern himself with inviting new settlers to a half-empty Jerusalem. And only after 1115 did he become free to direct attention to opportunities in his own realm. He took Montreal and Karak south and southeast of the Dead Sea and made them fortresses of great strategical importance. These two fortresses controlled a large barony, intercepting the profitable pilgrimage and caravan routes to Mecca and Egypt. He reached Ailat on the Red Sea and in 1118 attempted an invasion of Egypt with only 200 knights and

CHAPTER 2

400 footmen. But, in spite of initial success, the overtaxed barons and knights forced him to abandon this campaign. Fatally wounded, he was carried home.

Considering that his successor, Baldwin II (1118-1131), also fought most of his battles in northern Syria, first in an attempt to rectify the disastrous results of the slaughter of almost all of the Norman army by Il-Gazi of Mardin in 1119, then falling prisoner in Turkish hands while trying to save Edessa, and yet twice attacking Damascus (1126-1129) and Aleppo, one can hardly avoid the conclusion that the crusaders' involvement in northern Syria was the Achilles' heel of Jerusalem. It dispersed their limited resources and imposed on them insurmountable strategical conditions. Ultimately, this overambitiousness prevented them from forming realistic alliances with any of the contending forces in the area.

By the beginning of the second decade of the crusaders' history, close diplomatic relations with their neighbors and adjustments to the realities of Syrian politics resulted in a certain interlockage of the Christian principalities in a larger system. In the words of H.A.R. Gibb, "The dynasties of the crusading states were, unconsciously but effectively, absorbed into the system of Syrian politics, with its shifting play of alliances and counter-alliances, temporary treaties, sudden realignments, and petty gains and losses." To understand the fundamentals of this interlockage we must now look at the international system as a whole.

There was the "inner circle," with a juxtaposition of Christian strongholds on the Mediterranean coast and parallel Moslem principalities on the adjacent interior. In the north there lay a Christian projection stretching along the lines of the fertile crescent across the Euphrates, where the Frankish principality of Edessa established itself upon an Armenian and Syrian Christian base. In the south, the lower part of the territory of Jerusalem was flanked by Askalon on the seashore and the upper part was flanked by Damascus. The Kingdom had, at certain points, a width extending to the eastern and southern deserts. The Christian communication chain lay on the coast, from Acre via Tripoli to Antioch. On the other hand, between Damascus and Aleppo was a line of fortified towns: Baalbek, Homs, Hamah, Shaizar, and other fortresses constituting a direct communication chain. These small Arab powers were ruled by local emirs and inclined to intrigues based upon particularistic interests. To complete the picture, one must also consider the plurality of ethnic groups and religious sects, both Moslem and Christian.

But the balance-of-power politics involved an "outer circle" which included Iraqian, Byzantine, and Egyptian powers, as well as maritime forces from Italy. These powers saw intervention in Syrian affairs as a means of furthering their wider scope of interests. Beginning with the second decade of the crusaders' history, Syrian affairs were mainly influenced by the Mesopotamian Turks (i.e. the Saljuqid rulers of Mosul who were associated with the sultan and caliph of Bagdad), although all others in the "outer circle" were present and active from time to time.

Now let us examine briefly three typical alignments of parties in the "inner circle" as related to the extended system of international relations:

AN ALL-SYRIAN COALITION, MOSLEM AND CHRISTIAN, AGAINST IRAQ

This took place in 1115, when the Saljuqid Sultan of Iraq sent Bursuq ibn-Bursuq to "help" Aleppo against its neighbors. The ruler of Aleppo became so alarmed by his "savior" that he invited help from Tugtagin of Damascus, Il-Gazi the Ortuqid of Mardin, and—Roger of Antioch. The latter requested additional aid from Pons of Tripoli and Baldwin of Jerusalem. This solidarity of all Syrian princes, both Moslems and Christians, was not an expression of friendship or concern for Aleppo, of course; it reflected the common fear of the sultan of Bagdad. The coalition was rather ephemeral, but not insignificant. It resulted in

CHAPTER 2

Bursuq's final defeat by Roger at Danith, and in the opportunity for Baldwin to turn his initiative to southern Palestine. It also brought about some Moslem afterthoughts.

ALEPPO BECOMES A PROTECTORATE OF IRAQIAN POWERS

This was a process which began with mounting pressures from Antioch. In its early stages, the strong Shiite elements in Aleppo preferred limited subordination to the Franks to the certainty of liquidation by Sunnite Saljuqids. But the Normans of Antioch wanted a conquest, and did not refrain from constant plundering and even desecration of Moslem cemeteries. In 1119 Il-Gazi of Mardin with his Iraqian Turcomans accepted the protectorate of Aleppo and destroyed the Norman army in a major slaughter (known in Frankish history as *"ager sanguinis"*). In the third stage the Saljuqs of Mosul, under the ambitious Zangi, made Aleppo a center of their power (1128). Under the guise of a Jihad, Zangi used Aleppo both as a base from which to conduct independent politics in Iraq (aspiring even to power in Bagdad) and as a springboard to the occupation of Moslem and Christian Syria. Thus, local conflicts in the inner circle provided empire builders from the outer circle with the opportunity of subordinating Syrian affairs to foreign interests.

DAMASCUS MAKES ALTERNATE ALLIANCES AGAINST FRANKISH AND IRAQIAN AGGRESSION

As Aleppo turned to Iraq so Damascus turned to Egypt for cooperation against Frankish expansion. There had been some contact with the Egyptians as early as Baldwin I's time, but none as significant as this one. It was prompted by an attack on Askalon and Tyre (the yet-unconquered Arab coastal towns) in 1123-1124. While Baldwin II was imprisoned in Iraq, his army defeated the Egyptians on land, and the Venetian navy (according to an earlier agreement with Baldwin II) destroyed an Egyptian fleet near Jaffa. Tyre was conquered in 1124, after a long siege, and Damascus lost its last access to the sea. By 1126 Damascus was desperately in need of help against encroachments from Jerusalem, and sought aid from the Assassins, an activist Shiite organization that was being expelled from Aleppo. The Assassins received various concessions from Damascus, including the fortress of Banyas on the border with Jerusalem, in return for their help. Significantly, this alliance with the Assassins took place shortly after Baldwin II had attacked Damascus, inflicting heavy casualties upon its army. Then, in 1129, Baldwin II organized a second major attack on Damascus. This time he had reinforcements from Europe (the arrival of the first recruits for the newly established Order of the Temple, and Prince Fulk of Anjou, who came to marry the king's daughter), in addition to help from the Assassins whom he had persuaded to turn against the new rulers in Damascus. The major plan failed, however, and only Banyas was taken by the Franks. To contain Baldwin's expansion Damascus turned to Zangi in Aleppo (1130), but not at the cost of being conquered by him. Zangi was over-confident and ruthless. He seized Hamah by imprisoning its ruler, Savinj (son of the Damascus ruler, Bori), together with Damascus officers who came to his camp as allies. He was soon marching on Homs. The threat to Damascus was removed temporarily by Zangi's involvement in the struggle for the sultanate in Bagdad (1131). Now the ground was prepared for an alliance between the Franks and Damascus against the rising power of Zangi in the Mosul-Aleppo axis.

These selected developments indicate some of the basic intersections between the inner and outer circles of international relations. Local Syrian affairs were dynamically affected by these intersections. That is, inner balances could be disturbed or restored through some active intrusion of a peripheral party. At times no peripheral power was in a position to interfere. These were occasions for inner realignments or for the establishment of small kingdoms in the area. At other times one major power from the outer circle would be free to impose a certain order to the advantage or disadvantage of some inner party. Finally, there were rivalries between several peripheral forces, all trying to manipulate local units and being in turn instrumental to them. The result of this was, among other things, that political survival in the inner circle depended on the ability to foresee and utilize movements from the periphery. In other words: countervailing an unfavorable external interference was an existential *sine qua non* of regional politics.[10]

In the light of the above, it seems quite clear that even during the period of successful expansion the full scope of international relations in the area was only dimly grasped by the Franks. They had no realistic long-range policy. Their military expansions were dangerously opportunistic, and, except for their systematic establishment in the coastal cities, they wasted themselves in northern Syria. The persistence of imperial dreams is indicated in the fantastic title, "Kings of Babylonia and Asia," which the kings of Jerusalem assumed. Their involvement in Syrian politics stimulated Moslem realignments with powers in the outer circle (Iraq and Egypt). But, most significantly, the crusaders antagonized their natural ally Byzantium from the outset. They also neglected the possibility of forming a durable association with Italians such as the Normans of Sicily for example. This perfect isolationism coupled with their dispersion in four principalities, threatening practically every single state in the region—large or small, inner or outer—contained the seeds of their future failures.

[10] This characterization seems true of all times, including the present, *mutatis mutandis*.

Institutional Lag and Innovative Functions

Institutionally Known Ways of Meeting Political Necessities

Our historical survey might have created the false impression of containing within itself a sufficient explanation for the developments in question. Was it not this or that individual or group whose policies and actions had such and such consequences? Certainly the chain of events was related to what the interacting participants thought, felt, and did. But precisely why certain ideas occurred and certain actions prevailed is what remains to be explained.

At the basis of the crusaders' divided goals and unrealistic dreams lie socio-cultural factors of a compulsive character. Before attempting a systematic examination of these factors, let us illustrate our point in a preliminary way. European feudal institutions established a direct dependence of military capacity upon the number of fief-holding knights. The crusaders, therefore, in the face of numerically superior enemies, strove desperately to acquire more land in order to maintain a sufficiently large military establishment. Their eagerness to expand reflected both a political necessity and an institutional compulsion. The Normans and Franks were only dimly aware of the system in which they became interlocked. They had to choose realistically between crushing the main centers of power in the Middle East, and entrenching themselves in a compact maritime principality which would depend on extra-feudal resources. For the first alternative they lacked sufficient manpower, and for the second they had such institutional (i.e. mental) barriers as their European heritage imposed on them.

CHAPTER 3

Aside from the inability to realize their dreams of expansion, the crusaders faced a total threat to their very existence. Thus, in their hostile environment the loose federation of Latin principalities was forced to maintain unconventionally large armies just for defensive purposes. Yet they lacked sufficient agricultural land to maintain this kind of an army. So small a territory requiring so large an army was a social and political abnormality from the vantage point of European feudalism. And, besides the external threat to their existence, there was the usual internal conflict of claims over princely and baronial status. One must keep in mind the mobile situation of those crusaders who remained in the east. Many of them were devoid of established positions in Europe, and those of relatively high ranks aspired to still higher ones.[1] Success in the competition for political supremacy among the various leaders of crusading groups ultimately depended on the size of their armies. Territorial expansion was their only institutionally known way to support such armies and thus achieve status. Consequently, the whole Levant was treated as if it were an open frontier. The military vacuum which existed at the advent of the First Crusade had shaped this image, and the somewhat misleading successes of the first decade reinforced it. However, the crusaders were soon caught in a much more complicated situation than their wishful thinking had led them to believe, a situation with far-reaching international implications, the fundamentals of which were explained in the previous chapter.

Thus it can be seen that institutional patterns underlie and, to a degree, explain policies and actions. This is another way of saying that the functions of a given social structure determine a significant proportion of human goals and the means used for their attainment. To understand these functions is to gain a measure of predictability of actions and their consequences. If, however, by considering actions in the context of their social functions one can

[1] J. Prawer, *A History of the Latin Kingdom of Jerusalem*, Vol. I (The Bialik Institute, 1963), 355-56.

detect significant causes of events, it seems reasonable to assume that by considering social functions *themselves* in the context of their inter-societal conditions one might render historical events still more intelligible.

The method being followed here consists, then, in an attempt to answer three basic questions:

1) What were the significant *differences* between the two phases of inter-societal existence of the crusaders?

2) What tendencies or resistance to institutional change were manifested in that transplanted society?

3) What relevant connections may be established between international systems and social structures in the case in question?

Two Phases of Inter-societal Existence

In his profound analysis of the emergence of vassalage, Marc Bloch treated it as an adaptational innovation in the *protective* function of communities at a time when neither the state nor kinship groups provided adequate protection. "In yielding thus to the necessities of the moment these generations of men had no conscious desire to create new social forms, nor were they aware of doing so. Instinctively each strove to turn to account the resources provided by the existing social structure and if, unconsciously, something new was eventually created, it was in the process of trying to adapt the old."[2] In our sociological terminology, "trying to adapt the old" when it is no longer adequate is termed *institutional lag*, while "creating new social forms" in this context involves an adaptive modification of social functions which we call *innovative functions*. These concepts, general as they may be, are useful in analyzing the process of feudalization in its distinctly European form. They may also provide an analytical point of departure for understanding the conditions under which feudalism itself came to represent an institutional lag.

If it was the *protective* function of state and kinship

[2] Marc Bloch, *Feudal Society* (tr. by L. A. Manyon) (University of Chicago Press, 1961), p. 148.

that the institution of vassalage gradually replaced, then feudalism as a form of social organization cannot be adequately understood without reference to changing intersocietal relations. Indeed, whether we consider the collapse and fragmentation of the Carolingian empire, or the successive network of independent principalities under the Holy Roman Empire and the early Capetian kings, down to the autonomous groupings of lords and vassals entrenched in defensible castles and subsiding on the labor of subordinated village communities—in all of the above we can see that vassalage gained predominance in regulating man-to-man relations by virtue of its capacity to control community-to-community relations. The devastating invasions of Moslems, Vikings, and Magiars into western Europe during the 9th and 10th centuries played a key role in the process of feudalization. In the absence of a money economy and effective administration and communication system, these challenging circumstances increased the functional importance of the knightly class, whose remuneration in benefices initiated the process of territorial decentralization. As anarchy and insecurity increased, the monopoly of armored, mounted warriors over the means of warfare was transformed into a more or less complete control of the means of subsistence, and through it over the entire social structure. This growing preponderance of the knightly class could succeed only at the expense of a class-transcending central authority, such as a state or a church. It rested on the personal solidarity of groups of warriors in collective defense of their properties, these being identical with their concept of political territory.[3] Thus external threats from invasions were intensified by internal "civil wars" among various claimants of power. As one historian puts it, it was "the heyday of the soldier. No village, cathedral, city, or

[3] This is well illustrated by Marc Bloch (*ibid.*, p. 444): "We want lands, said in effect the Norman lords who refused the gifts of jewels, arms and horses offered by their Duke. And they added among themselves: 'it will thus be possible for us to maintain many knights, and the Duke will no longer be able to do so. . . .'"

monastic establishment was safe unless adequately protected by armed men. . . . The simple knight who had just enough land and peasant labor to support him and his family was the vassal of a larger land-holder, who in turn would be the vassal of a still mightier man."[4] However, such hierarchies were discontinuous in the sense that they did not weld together the former empire upon the ruins of which they arose; neither did they eliminate at once violence and disorder on the regional level. In time the independent principality became the basic political unit of the feudal system, and vassalage regulated both intra-principality and inter-principality relations. Thus, although the feodo-vassalic relations facilitated the process of political fragmentation, they also prevented complete disintegration.[5] These regional-personal groupings assumed sovereignty because they proved effective in resisting violent intrusions from without, and they gained the exclusive control and loyalty of their working population because they established peace and order within their limited territory. They were an alternative to anarchy. Of course, the institutions of vassalage and serfdom depended on the collaboration of older institutions, such as religion, the manor, and kinship, as well as upon ethnic identities and traditions. In other words, they operated within the traditions of a civilization with common integrating characteristics. But feudalism determined the social structure precisely because of the weakness (i.e. lag) of older institutions, including religion, in contributing to the protective function, namely, to inter-societal relations. The Church preceded feudalism and survived it, but had to reinforce feudalism and adapt to it before it could play any role in mitigating its brutalities or imbuing it with religious values. The extent to which the Church as a civilizational institution under feudalism influenced inter-societal relations was conditioned by its own feudalization,

[4] Sidney Painter, *A History of the Middle Ages* (Knopf, 1954), pp. 104-06.
[5] François L. Ganshof, *Le Moyen Age*, in Pierre Renouvin (ed.), *Histoire Des Relations Internationales*, Vol. I (Paris, 1953), p. 57.

including the merger of values and ideals, and by its capacity to act as a political entity. In turn, the extent to which the Church contributed later to the transformation of feudalism depended on the degree to which it preserved non-feudal cultural elements. What is true of religion as a social institution is also true, *mutatis mutandis*, of the state (or monarchy), the economy, kinship, and other cultural spheres. They were all transformed by the structure of feodo-vassalic power on the inter-societal as well as on the intra-societal level. Only such changes that would weaken the monopoly of the ruling class of warriors over the means of warfare, or disturb its balance of power and its political dispersion could pave the way to other forms of social organization.

By the 11th century the core institution of the feudal principality as a basic political unit of western European civilization (vassalage) had acquired two faces: one directed outward to the control of principality-to-principality relations, and one oriented inward to the regulation of man-to-man relations. It became a well-balanced and functioning system, although not without structural instabilities of its own. According to one historian, "In theory, the feudal system furnished means for the peaceful settlement of all disputes between a lord and his vassals, and between vassals of the same lord. All such disputes could be heard in the lord's court. There was no provision for quarrels between vassals of different lords and these could only be settled by negotiation or war. Actually the practice did not follow theory very closely. . . . Only as the great lords—kings and feudal princes—became overwhelmingly strong in the late 12th and 13th centuries were they able to reduce materially the amount of feudal warfare by exercising their rights as suzerains."[6] However, even before the formation of strong monarchies, the feudal dispersion of power, its undeveloped technology, the relaxation of alien invasions, combined with religious and cultural checks, all contributed

[6] Sidney Painter, *ibid.*, p. 114.

to the predominance of conjunctive rather than disjunctive inter-societal relations within western Europe. To mention just the combination of vassalic customs and military technology, it was sufficient for a lord to own and garrison a castle, in which he could resist attack for forty days, in order to retain his power and government in the surrounding region. As was pointed out earlier, the fundamental characteristic of a feudal army was its not being an instrument in the hands of a state, but operating rather as a ruling class in collective defense of its properties, these being identical with a politically autonomous territory. The internal balance of power of each feodo-vassalic aggregation as well as its solidarity guaranteed that its supreme but equal ruler (be he king, duke, count, or baron) shall depend upon his fief-holding men for power, and that he conform to customary feudal limitations in the exercise of authority. Yet, the functions of leadership and administration in a feudal principality were divided between two distinct needs: inner solidarity and foreign relations. On the one hand, much as the inner solidarity of the knightly class rested on the institution of vassalage, there remained a certain "free military market" in which violent competition could develop, and thus leadership was needed to mitigate the self-destructive potentialities of the social structure. On the other hand, leadership on the level of relations with other societies implied a potential distinction between the knightly class and a class-transcending framework (i.e. a state), which could lead to direct subordination of personal power to state authority. Indeed, each feudal principality contained some elements of a state, such as a high court in which vassals as peers performed judicial, legislative, and executive functions (originating as a *duty* to give council and developing into a *right* to do so),[7] a centralized conduct of diplomacy, alliances and treaties with other principalities, coinage and the regulation of inter-societal trade, extra-feudal franchises to non-agricultural groups and their legal

[7] J. Prawer, *ibid.*, p. 385.

protection, and last but not least, its not-altogether-feudal articulation with monasteries and church personnel.

However, two general aspects of the feudal principality must be emphasized in order to grasp its particular form of viability. *Internally*, it rested on the class supremacy and solidarity of specialized warriors integrated by personalized ties of obedience and protection (vassalage), on the balanced distribution of power and income in service tenements instead of salary (the fief), and on the exploitation of peasant communities (serfdom). *Externally*, it existed as an integral part of a wider inter-societal system welded together by common institutions in addition to vassalage, namely, by religious uniformity, political compatibility, and mutual recognition. In feudal theory, principalities were linked to a common suzerain, but in reality they just coexisted with him. Yet in case of war, even if confronted by superior forces, the principality did not face total annihilation, or a major uprooting of people. So long as it operated as a co-existing sub-unit within the confines of the above-characterized system (not beyond its frontiers!) the viability of the feudal principality was guaranteed, regardless of shifts in political affiliations.

Admittedly, the above discussion omits significant differences between countries of western Europe (France, Germany, England, Italy) as well as regional variations within these countries. Also no precise definition was offered as to the scope and boundaries of the inter-societal system under consideration, or the nature of its foreign relations with other systems. Nevertheless, this "ideal type" of feudalism (with all its accentuations and omissions) corresponds, it is hoped, to historical reality in terms of the specific problems investigated in this study.

We have examined the social and political environment of the crusaders before their transplantation. We have treated social structure as a function of inter-societal structure. We have seen how the functional interlockage of societies established a historically evolved inter-societal system reaching deep into the core of "internal" social institutions, and how the latter depend for their stability and viability upon a typically adequate discharge of inter-societal functions. Let us now turn to problems associated with transplantation.

So far we have followed the process of feudalization from its emergence as an innovative function to its attainment of historical stability. The potentiality of structural instability was indicated, although not elaborated. Before doing this, it must be pointed out that stability itself may produce cumulative changes which eventually become a source of crisis and instability. For example, if under favorable conditions stability facilitates economic growth which, in turn, accelerates population increase but lags behind it, a crisis may arise undermining the very stability which initiated the whole process. According to the Malthusian model this is a general and recurrent crisis which is usually resolved by war. This hypothesis about the social consequences of population surplus is far from being universally confirmed if we examine various types of inter-societal systems comparatively and historically. There were wars without population surpluses, and there were population surpluses without wars. Certain social structures, however, are definitely predisposed to expansion in various forms including warfare. Such seems to be the case with the European feudal system from approximately the 11th century on. It is probably not an accident that demographic and economic growth were associated with the growing vitality of feudalism and with the extension of its boundaries in various directions. Without delving into the intricacies of how these factors initially reacted upon one another, or of the commercial, cultural, and political developments in Europe which followed into the 12th and 13th centuries, let us focus on the structural predispositions of the knightly class in the second half of the 11th century, since these are more relevant to our investigation.

More than any other segment, the knightly class experienced a manpower surplus at the time. In proportion to the success in achieving security and balance through vassalage, the ruling aristocracy of feudal Europe kept producing professional lords without lands and knights without benefactory lords. Despite the increase of the peasant population and the extension of agricultural cultivation, the demand for benefices and fiefs exceeded the supply. One reason for this was that the right to be a knight was not yet a hereditary privilege, and thus the class as a whole expanded by mobility from below in addition to reproduction. On the other hand, the status of knight, once achieved, was not likely to be lost, as the stratification system tightened and "free men" had to choose between ascending to knighthood and sinking into serfdom. Among the higher ranks of the nobility, equal inheritance of power and wealth by several sons and daughters could only lead to unlimited fragmentation of territories, and therefore primogeniture became one of the solutions to this problem. Younger sons of the upper ranks and disadvantaged knights of the lower ranks had one main response to their predicament: acquisition or conquest of new land, i.e. land available for peaceful colonization or inhabited land vulnerable to enforced subjection. The alternative of entering other occupations was inconceivable under the given stratification system, except for ecclesiastic careers which, indeed, were often acquired through "investiture" by powerful relatives.[8] Of course, as the bottleneck at the top of the feudal pyramid grew narrower, acute competition could easily intensify the civil wars. But the growing political stability and balance of the feudal system coupled with the influence of the Church (after the Cluniac reforms) encouraged the land-hungry to look to the frontiers of feudal Europe rather than to its strongholds in the interior. Given the extreme weakness of feudal monarchy, the problem as well as the initiative in solving it remained in the hands of feodo-vassalic groupings on the sub-principality level. It is these power- and

[8] Baldwin I, King of Jerusalem, for example, pursued priestly opportunities before joining the Crusade. Another alternative was to join the household of an established lord if he could use and support more knights, or if he was embarking upon an adventurous expedition.

land-hungry groups that made history on the frontiers of feudal Europe and shaped its initial expansions.[9]

Since our concern here is to analyze the crusaders' society in transplantation and not feudal expansion in general, let us just briefly distinguish it from the others as a type. It seems reasonable to distinguish three types of feudal European expansion: peaceful, sponge-like absorption, military boundary-extension, and overseas colonization. The first may be illustrated by the movement of enterprising lords with induced working manpower into uncultivated areas of the interior or the frontier where, by forest clearing, new feudal settlements were established. The second took the form of military expeditions against neighboring peoples, such as the "crusades" against the yet unconverted Slavs and other central and eastern European tribes, the conquests of England, southern Italy, and Sicily by the Normans, and the thrusts into Spain. It was the availability of free virgin land and the pressing demand for it which enabled the first movement, and it was the relative vulnerability of the adjacent peoples which facilitated the second movement. The *common aspect of both types was their proximity to the centers of feudal civilization and the possibility of acculturation of those marginal areas and peoples.* The advantage of overwhelming reinforcement and pressure from the close-by hinterland of feudalism proved decisive in these expansions. Finally, the newly founded political units in these annexed areas could be effectively incorporated into the institutionalized inter-societal system of European feudalism, and thus benefit from its stability, vitality, balances, and security.[10]

[9] A. R. Lewis, "The Closing of the Mediterranean Frontier," *Speculum* (October 1958); see also W. D. Wyman and C. B. Kroeber (eds.), *The Frontier in Perspective* (University of Wisconsin Press, 1957), pp. 26-34.

[10] The point made here is not that the imported feudalism of Norman England, Sicily, or other partly feudalized areas, such as Italy, Spain, and central Europe, did not differ in form from the original feudalism of western Europe. There were factors that made for significant differences. However, *their international conditions of existence did not change significantly.*

CHAPTER 3

While the filling in of uncultivated areas and the military expansion into the adjacent frontiers did not amount to a real detachment from the European inter-societal environment, it was otherwise with the overseas expansion of the crusaders. We have described at length the characteristics of the feudal principality in relation to its inter-societal conditions. We have seen how its social organization evolved in response to these conditions and how the functionality of its established institutions was relative to the particular mode of feudal coexistence. Now we can ask what might happen if one of these feodo-vassalic units, namely, that "ruling class in collective action," migrates far beyond the frontier, where it becomes interlocked with hostile rivals bent on its total annihilation.

It appears that the immediate result with respect to the institution of vassalage would be contradictory or paradoxical in nature. In foreign relations its functional importance might practically disappear, since the participants in this international system have incompatible aims and ideologies (at least vis-à-vis a foreign intruder) and do not recognize one another's right to exist. Internally, however, vassalage would gain in strength, since the functional importance of the knightly class would have to increase as warfare intensified. Again, paradoxically, the acute demand for fighting manpower would tend to open the ranks of knighthood to mobility from below, but the religious and ethnic differences of the native population would make it impossible. Thus the knightly class would be automatically converted into a legal caste with religion and ethnicity as a rigid dividing line between it and the subjected working population. Its complete monopoly over the means of warfare and its feodo-vassalic solidarity would stand firmly in the way of any legal reform or centralizing efforts of a king intent on mobilizing extra-feudal resources and manpower. If the number of knights shrunk as a result of excessive warfare, diminishing the occupied territories would be no safe remedy (as it would be at home) in the face of incessantly encroaching enemies. The Kingdom would desperately need reinforcements from the homeland, but it would have very poor material incentives to offer them. On the other hand, even if reinforcements did come but the size of territories shrunk as a result of enemy occupations, the Kingdom would lack lands and income to sustain them. These in fact were only a few of the peculiarities and problems faced by the transplanted society of the crusaders in its new political environment.

When the Normans and Franks encountered another migratory ruling class, the Saljuqs, on the eastern coast of the Mediterranean, the situation was naturally adverse to the Latins. The military tactics of the Saljuqs were based on numerical superiority and on the swift movements of their light cavalry, which was capable of shooting arrows while in motion. The heavy cavalry of the Franks had the advantage only in pitched battles where they could win by virtue of the sheer weight of their famous charge with spears. But this difference gave the Saljuqs more freedom in choosing the time and place of battles, as they learned from experience the strengths and weaknesses of the enemy. Thus the Latins had to protect the bodies of their horses by surrounding them with foot soldiers and keep their military formations relatively immobile until an opportunity for a charge arose. The Saljuqid hosts could make not only swift changes in tactical formations, but could replace their casualties more easily from the reserves of nomadic Turcoman tribes.[11] Moreover, the Saljuqs as a recently Islamized class of warriors assumed the role of "defenders of the faith," thus mobilizing various segments of the population to support their legitimate struggle against Christian aggression. As if these odds were not sufficient, the grand ambitions of the crusaders induced them to occupy widely separated positions in Syria and the Holy Land, which entangled them with vital interests of three empires: Byzantium, the Abassids of Iraq, and the Fatimids of Egypt. These

[11] For a detailed analysis of the military history of the crusades in its social and political contexts, see R. Smail, *Crusading Warfare* (Cambridge University Press, 1956).

CHAPTER 3

powers (as explained in the historical survey) could not fail to envisage what the conquest of Syria and the Holy Land by Europeans would mean to their own future.

Now, if it is true, as it has often been said, that European feudal society was "organized for war," it is even more true that it was adapted to war on its own terms, namely, to institutionalized inter-princely or inter-baronial skirmishes conducted in fixed seasons. It did not require and was not capable of prolonged large-scale military enterprises, which go hand in hand with elaborate, centralized governments. Thus the political and military circumstances of transplantation to the Middle East could be favorable to the crusaders only to the extent that some comparable political fragmentation prevailed there. However, the very intrusion of the Latins deep into the domains of Islamic civilization encouraged the restoration of political unity and antagonistic affiliations there.

It is against this background that one can better understand the political predicaments and institutional lags of the crusaders.

Tendencies and Resistance to Institutional Change

It seems that the most farsighted colonization program with which the Franks could meet their critical international conditions and possibly prevent destruction consisted in the following measures:

1) create an all-Christian Franko-Syrian society to inhabit and defend with sufficient manpower the Holy Land;

2) develop a substantial maritime strength on the commercial base of the coastal towns to carry on extensive trade between European and eastern countries and to buttress the military establishment;

3) complete the trend manifested in the frontier communities of the religio-military orders, which integrated religious, military, and economic functions in order to establish a strong centralized monarchy with a standing army at its disposal.

Lest the above program seem as merely retroactive wisdom on the part of an observer, it must be pointed out that these ideas were, in fact, contemplated and partly implemented by the Franks, as we shall presently see. However, each of these tendencies implied a sharp departure from the entrenched social order. Hence their eventual indecisiveness and insufficiency. What follows is a characterization of these tendencies as incongruent social innovations.

The first item involved attracting Christian Syrians of various sects to settle in the Kingdom of Jerusalem. In terms of numbers, these native Christians (Greek Orthodox, Maronites, Nestorians, Jacobites, and Armenians) were ten times greater than the Frankish and Italian elements combined. Although most of them had settled to the north of Palestine, they were naturally inclined to seek protection and cooperation from Christian governments. A policy in this direction was initiated by Baldwin I. In 1115 he invited all Syrians and Christian Arabs from Transjordan to settle on his own estates in Jerusalem. He offered them, and even Moslem tradesmen, attractive commercial franchises. But this policy was not effectively pursued by successive rulers. A special interest was maintained in the Armenians, however, due to their military capacity (able-mounted warriors) and their political status (semi-independent principalities). Thus, beginning with Baldwin II, who married the Armenian Morphia, the royal dynasty of Jerusalem became half Armenian. But the aristocracy as a whole did not follow this example and preferred to preserve its European exclusiveness. Still more significant was the religious ethnocentrism of the Latin Church. When Thoros II, a powerful Armenian prince, offered to transfer 30,000 Armenian warriors with their families to the Kingdom of Jerusalem, King Amalric and the barons were interested, but the Church undermined the negotiations. It refused to grant them equal religious status and to exempt them from paying the "dime" tax. Hostility toward the Syrian Christians from the outset is reflected in a letter from one of the participants in the conquest of Antioch: "We have expelled the Turks and the pagans, but as to the heretics, Greeks and Armenians, Syrians and Jacobites, we were unable to chase them out."[12] We know of a rapprochement between the Maronites of Lebanon and the Latin Church, but also of their mass slaughter in Tripoli by Raymond II in revenge for collaboration with Damascus. On the whole, Christian Syrians were at best tolerated by the Franks, but never treated as equals, and no imaginative policy of colonization was applied to them. The potentiality of a Franko-Syrian society in the land holy to all Christians was not realized. Consequently, they remained marginal groups between Moslems and Franks, and were forced to cooperate with both in that defensive expediency typical of oppressed minorities.[13] Even if most Christian Syrians lacked the asset of a military tradition, the Franks could not afford to alienate them in the face of Islamic preponderance in the area. But this cooperation fell far short of founding a Franko-Syrian society, which was made virtually impossible by the discriminating and rigid monopoly of the Latin Church. A class structure, based on ascriptive categories of status and sanctified by religion and ethnic exclusiveness, was the central social institution of the Kingdom of Jerusalem. Its political and economic superstructure could not transcend the base which shaped it. The only way institutionally known to the Franks of incorporating new social elements was by establishing alien lordships over useful villagers, craftsmen, and traders.

As to the second possibility, namely, of commercial and maritime development, a more definite implementation of policy was the case. The Italian naval powers of Genoa, Pisa, and Venice played a decisive role in the conquest of

[12] Hagenmeyer (ed.), *Lettres de Croisades*, quoted by Claude Cahen, *La Syrie du Nord à L'Epoque Des Croisades* (Librairie Orientaliste Paul Geuthner, 1940), p. 333, who remarks: "This 'we are unable' does not seem charged with kindness . . ."

[13] When Bishop Basil of Edessa was asked by the Moslem conquerors if he would make a reliable citizen, he replied that his previous loyalty to the Franks proved how faithful he could be. S. Runciman, *A History of the Crusades*, Vol. II (Cambridge University Press, 1957), 237.

INSTITUTIONAL LAG & INNOVATIVE FUNCTIONS

the coastal towns, and special concessions were granted to them by the Kingdom. As a result of these agreements, Italian communes of tradesmen sprang up at Jaffa, Acre, Tyre, Beirut, Tripoli, and other ports. They had their judicial, economic, and religious self-rule; but, obviously, they also served the Kingdom in organizing income from the ports, in populating and defending them, and in providing the know-how for maritime commerce. Typically, the Kingdom "feudalized" some aristocratic Italians by granting them fiefs, as in the case of the Embriaco family of Genoa, which held the town of Gibelet in the north and ruled the colony in Acre. (This rich family gradually severed its ties and obligations to the mother city of Genoa and struck roots in the Levant.[14]) But instead of utilizing this available manpower and know-how for the development of a Jerusalemite maritime power, the covetous barons of Jerusalem exploited it. By the middle of the 12th century there were already noticeable disputes and violations of agreements between Italian merchants and the Frankish rulers, and between Italian colonists and their mother cities, which kept pressing for taxes with the aid of friendly popes.[15] The question arises, however, as to whether the Franks of Palestine were not ideally situated for playing a key role in the rising trade between Europe and the East, in addition to, or after the model of Italian commerce. This would have augmented both their military and economic achievements. As the Normans of Sicily did without a maritime tradition, so could the Franks build a strong navy of their own and thus solidify their international prominence and strategical positions. Yet, except for a very eccentric lord, Gerard of Sidon, who succeeded in building a "navy"

[14] Louis J. Paetow (ed.), *The Crusaders and Other Historical Essays* (F. S. Croft, 1928), pp. 145-49.

[15] W. Heyd, *Histoire du Commerce du Levant* (tr. by Furcy Raynaud), 2 vols. (Leipzig, 1936), pp. 158-61: "The commercial communities established in Syria were involved in a continuous struggle with the kings and ecclesiastical and lay dignitaries of the country in order to defend their goods, their rights, and their liberty."

of fifteen vessels, some negligible maritime achievements of Antioch, Tripoli, and the Orders, and the Red Sea naval adventures of Reynald of Chatillon, no substantial progress in this direction was attained. There are various opinions as to the commercial opportunities of the Kingdom. Some experts point out that in the 12th century Italian merchants had very little use for the liberal concessions granted to them by the Franks, since the main trade routes led to Egypt and Byzantium.[16] However, the emergency interest of the Franks in seapower, coupled with the available Genoese, Venetian, and Marseillesian colonies of Palestine and the special ties with pilgrims and markets in western Europe, should have insured some success in this direction. The kings of Jerusalem could certainly learn something from the example of Sicily and even from the Italian cities themselves, which, similarly, were pressed to the coast and surrounded by numerically superior neighbors. But this would have amounted to an alliance between the king and the urban commercial strata against the vested interests of the landed aristocracy. Also, the fact that the Jerusalemite knights themselves lived in towns rather than in dispersed rural castles prevented the formation of socially segregated, but politically strong, urban communities.

If the two preceding adaptational tendencies were clearly incongruent social innovations, the rise of the Hospitallers and Templars was deeply rooted in the monastic and knightly ideals of European feudalism. The *combination* of the two, however, was an original development in the Kingdom of Jerusalem. Here was a revolutionary synthesis of knighthood, of religious asceticism and collectivism, of frontier colonization, and of socio-political organization, both anchored in traditional institutions and transcending them at the same time.

Initially, the movement started simply as a response to the welfare needs of pilgrims on the one hand and to their

[16] Claude Cahen, "Notes sur l'Histoire des Croisades et de l'Orient Latin," *Bulletin de la Faculté des Lettres de Strasbourg* (1951), pp. 328-46.

INSTITUTIONAL LAG & INNOVATIVE FUNCTIONS

need for protection en route to Jerusalem on the other. Thus, the Hospital of St. John was originally a monastic order, living in Jerusalem by the Augustinian rule, bound by vows of poverty, chastity, and brotherhood, collecting alms for poor pilgrims and caring for the sick. They established "poor houses" for pilgrims in Jerusalem and in Europe. Baldwin I chartered them officially and confirmed their possessions. In 1112 the patriarch of Jerusalem and the archbishop of Caesaria exempted the Hospital from the payment of tithes. Patriarch Daimbert and King Baldwin bestowed lands and properties upon them as early as 1100, and their example was followed by nobles everywhere, so that their income and numbers increased rapidly. In 1113 came the Bull of Pope Paschal II, which confirmed their formation and granted them the privilege of electing their own Master and of operating without reference to the Church in Jerusalem. All this growth in activity, wealth, and status occurred before any military ideas were entertained by the Hospitallers.[17] Inspired perhaps by the example of the Hospitallers, a Knight of Burgundy, Hugh de Payens, together with eight other experienced crusaders, resolved to devote their lives to the duty of protecting the pilgrims on the Jaffa-Jerusalem road. They wanted to forsake worldly chivalry "of which human favor and not Jesus Christ was the cause" and form a religio-military community, living under the Benedictine rule. Baldwin II granted them quarters in a part of the royal palace next to the former Mosque Al-Aksa (Temple of Solomon) from which came their name, Knights of the Temple. This was the earliest known synthesis of the knight role with the monk role,[18] although at this early stage the Templars were mainly oc-

[17] E. G. King, *The Knights Hospitallers* (Methuen, 1931), p. 31.
[18] According to G. H. Campbell, *The Knights Templars* (Duckworth, 1937), pp. 21-22: ". . . a fighting force sworn to the church had never previously been known. . . . They were sworn servants of the Church, but servants sworn not to minister as priests to the people or to live as monks, passing their lives in prayer and meditation, but as soldiers whose duty was to honor God in fighting against the infidel." See also Marion Melville, *La Vie des Templiers* (Gallimard, 1957).

CHAPTER 3

cupied with providing armed escorts to pilgrims on the road and were not accorded a definite religious status.

It was not before 1127, in the Council of Troyes, led by St. Bernard, Abbot of Clairvaux, that the Order acquired a full-fledged ideology, a code of rules, and hundreds of recruits. These were, according to St. Bernard, the true "children of Israel" who could rely upon the Lord of the Sabbaoth; "one of them puts a thousand to flight and two of them ten thousand." St. Bernard's comparison of the secular knight with the Templars is classic and very informative. After describing the luxurious clothing and armor of the long-haired secular knights who throw themselves "recklessly and without thought" upon their enemy "not to achieve a noble purpose, but because of [their] savage hatred and [their] wild lust for glory and wealth," he goes on to say: "Let us now consider the soldiers of God. . . . They live together happily and temperately, and have neither wives nor children among them; and, so that nothing may be lacking for evangelical perfection, they live without property and share the same house . . . and it is as if one heart and one soul dwelleth in them all. They never sit idle or seek foolishly for news. When they are resting after their warfare against the infidels—and this is a thing that rarely happens—they employ their time in repairing their garments and weapons or in doing something which the Master commands or which is for the good of them all . . . this rather than eat the bread of idleness. There is no respect of persons among them. It is the best man, not the man of noblest birth, who is most highly prized. They try to outdo each other in respect and to bear one another's burdens. They shun games of chess and the gaming tables. They turn away from chase and from hawking in which others take so much pleasure. They hate all jugglers and mountebanks, and despise wanton songs and plays as vanities and follies of the world. They have their hair short in accordance with the words of the Apostle, 'It is not seemly in a man to have long hair.' They are never dressed up, they wash themselves seldom. Usually, they are covered with dust and are brown from the heat of the sun.

"When they go forth in battle they have faith within, and without they have weapons of iron. They never adorn themselves with gold, for they wish to strike terror in the enemy, not to arouse his desire for spoil . . . they do not rush madly and impetuously into the fray, but go carefully and prudently, coolly, like true children of Israel. But when the battle has begun, then they throw themselves unhesitatingly on their enemies, on whom they look as mere sheep. . . . They are joined in a peculiar union: they are at once meeker than lambs and more terrible than lions, so that one wonders whether they should be called monks or knights. They have the right to both names, for they possess the gentleness of the monk and the courage of the knight. What more need be said, except that this is the Lord's doing and is wonderous in our eyes. Such are the men whom God has chosen from out of the bravest in Israel, so that watchful and reliable, mighty with the sword and skilled in war, they may keep the Holy Sepulchre."[19]

Such was the original ideology of the Temple. Its leader and founder, Hugh de Payens, was officially supported by King Baldwin II, confirmed by the Pope, and ordained by the most influential Benedictine monk and spiritual leader in Europe. Consequently, the kings of France and England and many of their nobles endowed the Temple with estates to serve as recruiting and training preceptories, following the example of one member of the Council of Troyes. Gifts of money and lands also flowed into the hands of the organization from "associate members" who joined in the activities. Two years later, in 1129, 300 Knights Templars were operating as the equivalent of a standing army behind Baldwin II in his attack on Damascus; and, more significantly, they played a decisive role in the king's attack upon his own rebellious daughter, Alice of Antioch.

[19] Campbell, *ibid.*, pp. 30-32.

CHAPTER 3

About this time, the lambs of the Hospital of St. John were also ready to put on lions' skins. The militarization of the Hospital occurred in the late twenties, gradually at first, perhaps under the pressure of the security crises of those years, until revolutionized by their second Master, Raymond of Puy, another Burgundian nobleman. The transition was described as the result of a "divine call" to Raymond of Puy to "take the swords which they had flung aside when they entered the service" of the original monastic order; it was reinforced by a blessing from the patriarch of Jerusalem.

The Templars and the Hospitallers soon became an asset that any European monarch of the time might envy. Being far more dependable and certainly less expensive than any mercenary army, they established a completely new channel of mobility which reinforced the conventional knightly army. They tapped the European reservoir of proletarian knights and pilgrims. With capital collected in Europe as donations to the Holy Land, and with the spirit of ascetic Christian idealism, they could be entrusted with frontier castles and maintain in them self-sufficient communities, both economically and militarily. At the same time, these communities were committed to serve the Kingdom as disciplined and trained armies with numbers unlimited by the size of the estate, its income, or any feudal prearrangement. When conventional fiefs became highly insecure and profitless as a result of constant invasions and plunderings, these positions could be, and were indeed, handed over to the collective ownership and responsibility of the Orders. Thus the Orders may be considered as "non-profit" religio-military corporations, gradually filling the gaps created by retreating "private enterprises" of land-holding warriors, the barons and knights of Jerusalem. "Non-profit" refers, of course, to individual members of the Orders and not to the collective corporation, which could and did amass wealth in one place while being capable of using it elsewhere, even at a loss, when public consideration so required. No wonder that under the precarious international conditions of the Kingdom the Orders eventually became the backbone of the military establishments, taking over one castle after another and eventually controlling the most strategically located fortresses.

There is no doubt that a king with farsighted statesmanship could have employed this movement in two distinct but mutually supporting ways. Firstly, he could have embarked upon that type of intensive collectivized colonization which, as the Orders demonstrated, was most suitable to the special needs of the Kingdom. Secondly, he could have established a strong centralized monarchy, independent of conventional feudal services and their limitations, with the Orders as his standing army. Although the Orders constituted a living suggestion of the above, this "hypothetical revolution" never took place. We have seen how congruent this tendency was with respect to traditional ideals of this society. But congruence with social ideals is not necessarily congruence with traditional institutions. On this we need comment presently.

The Orders indeed were quite a perplexing phenomenon to all concerned, including their own leadership. For the first time a feudal nobility was confronted by monks who were also knights, a kind of "church-in-arms" with a military capacity equal or superior to the secular establishment. In the same way, the official conventional clergy was confronted for the first time by a military organization with inherent religious authority. As aptly characterized by St. Bernard, "They are joined in a peculiar union—so that one wonders whether they should be called monks or knights. They have the right to both names." Thus, they stood between two prominent segments of the ruling elite, combining qualities, claims, and obligations of both, and pointing to a most serious threat to the vested interests and ideology of both. Previously, there had been a feudal balance: the Church lacked coercive power, and the nobility lacked religious authority and independent legitimacy. Thus, they became interdependent as stated in the well-known feudal principle that "some work, some fight, and some pray." But

CHAPTER 3

the Orders possessed what either part of the elite lacked, for they could pose as an armed church or a Godly army. Moreover, by being situated between the king and the aristocracy as a whole, both secular and ecclesiastic, they created a dilemma for the king himself. On the one hand, the Orders were clearly an effective and invaluable response to the pressing security problem of the Kingdom; and they could also be used as a central tool to discipline feudal rebels, so that the king could hardly miss the vision of a viable government distinct and separate from the institution of vassalage. On the other hand, a feudal monarch still was, by his very mentality, the central symbol and pillar of feudal solidarity and not a natural leader of a theocratic state. It would have amounted to a fundamental revolution if the king chose to lean on "monastic collectivistic knighthood," especially when such knights were not vassals of the king, but rather sworn to the Pope, and somewhat unpredictable in their action. To transcend this dilemma was not a simple matter for any king accustomed to function as *primus inter pares* of a secular ruling class of which he himself was actually a member. Consequently, it was more congruent with the legal order to consider the Orders as just another type of barony and, indeed, a dangerously privileged one. To the ordinary baronies of the Franks, two special ones were added, then: the Templars and Hospitallers, headed by two grand Masters who participated in the supreme feudal body of political administration and legislation, the *Haute Cour*. They were not vassals of the king, however, but had a very special and autonomous status. The great power of this social movement was due to the fact that it grew from within the existing institutional order and was based on its most sanctified ideals. It was thus a culturally organic innovation. At the same time, it represented not utopian dreams but a rather adequate adaptation to the international conditions of existence, and, in fact, was responsible for prolonging the life of the Kingdom. However, this adaptational innovation, if synthesized with the centralizing interests of the king, contained the potentiality of breaking the monopoly of the secular knightly class over the means of warfare and of upsetting the official clerical establishment. Obviously, this trend was bound to meet with powerful built-in resistance.[20]

In time, the accommodation of the Orders to the feudal structure of their society transformed them into a special status group aspiring to closed ranks and accumulated properties; their initial revolutionary spirit was spent. They became a part of a legal knightly class based on hereditary qualifications for admission. They competed with barons of the aristocracy for power and conducted a foreign policy of their own. The kings could not control them effectively, and, fearing their tendency to independence, they overlooked the possibility of centralizing the monarchy through them. King Amalric came closest to doing so, both in legislation and in special alliance with the Orders. In his critical reign, most of the lands of the Kingdom, as well as the lands of Tripoli and Antioch, were divided between the Hospitallers and the Templars. The Templars became the king's rivals as well as bitter opponents of their twin Order. Regular feudal intrigues, in which the best interests of the Kingdom were not always at heart, resulted in political fragmentation in spite of the threat from the growing Islamic empire which engulfed it.

Inter-societal System and Social Structure

The rise of monastic-collectivistic knighthood in the Kingdom of Jerusalem cannot be adequately understood if interpreted as a function of a single social system considered in isolation. Nor would it suffice to refer simply to "other societies" as aspects of a general environment. The possibility of treating such "environments" as evolved systems of functionally interlocked societies must be pointed

---

[20] Purely secular collective bodies of knights existed in Europe, too—for example, the *milites castri* in Burgundy, or the Knights of the Arms of Nimes. Such groups were not usually helpful in the work of centralization. But no European state reached such a degree of dependence on these bodies as did the Kingdom of Jerusalem.

CHAPTER 3

out. These are wholes which influence not only relations among parts, but also the changing functions of pivotal social institutions. Thus, internal stratification may change in reference to new inter-societal conditions, and with it the entire social order may undergo some transformation.

Earlier in this study the experimental value of considering a transplanted society in a new mode of international existence was pointed out. Subsequently, the historical emergence of the Kingdom of Jerusalem was related to a field of international forces which permitted its consolidation. Once established, its course became interlocked with that of other societies, constituting a problematic condition of existence for one another. Our interest was then focused upon the differences between the two successive modes of international existence and the resulting effects upon social structure. Clearly, political relations under European feudalism were so institutionalized as to balance and stabilize decentralized structures based on vassalage and a backbone force of secular knighthood. In the Middle East, on the other hand, incompatible ideologies and an overwhelming threat to survival (among other factors) gradually pushed the European type of feudalism into a lag. We have described at length the interdependence between the feudal principality and its European inter-societal system, as well as the chronic crises and peculiarities of the Latin Kingdom in the East. If we are justified in assuming that the transplanted institutionalized order was relatively stable (a fact ascertained from comparable "control groups" of French feudalism of the 11th and 12th centuries, at least to the time of Philip Augustus), then its non-typical crisis in the discharge of social functions together with its adaptational innovations must be attributed to factors of the new inter-societal milieu.[21]

[21] It is definitely not claimed here that western European society remained stationary after the "crusaders" departure. However, the vitality and stability of its feudal institutions continued well into the 13th century and beyond, side by side with the cumulative development of commerce, a money-economy, towns, and the bourgeoisie, as well as

However, even a course of action which leads to the military collapse or destruction of a society is a form of social change. At any rate, to the extent that structural predispositions are responsible for this course, it is clearly an aspect of the connection between inter-societal systems and social structure. Thus the circumstances of our historical case correspond in principle to the requirements of controlled experiments in which a causal connection may be established between a changing independent variable (inter-societal system) and a dependent variable (social structure) while other factors are being controlled.

Of course, one case study can only contribute to the formation of a reasonable hypothesis; it cannot establish a theory. More comprehensive and systematic reference to empirical materials will be required for that. What we are attempting here is to indicate the *indispensability* of considering social structure and change in an inter-societal context. Let us restate concisely the fundamentals of this hypothesis in the light of our findings so far.

Students of social change might find the special case of the Kingdom of Jerusalem interesting in two respects: first, because of the charismatic fusion of contradictory roles in social movements oriented to the transformation of traditional institutions, as exemplified by the religio-military orders; second, because of the institutional lag and innovative functions in relation to inter-societal conflict rather than to technological advancement, which may be balanced on the inter-societal level. We may define institutional lag

---

intellectual and religious achievements. These were indeed changes which later became decisive in transforming European feudalism. Yet the development of a strong monarchy, however aided by centralizing interests of the bourgeoisie and the Church, represented mainly "imperialistic" expansion of one feudal principality at the expense of similar units and their mutual affiliation. All of the above extra-feudal factors are precisely what the transplanted society of the crusaders lacked under its inter-societal conditions. Therefore, its special crises (e.g. a chronic scarcity of knights and lands) were non-typical in relation to European feudalism. As with the peculiarity of challenges so with the peculiarity of response.

as the persistence of action patterns adapted to needs of the past resulting in minimal adaptational consequences under new situations. And innovative functions are associated with congruent or incongruent social innovations (with respect to a given institutional order) resulting in activities which have an optimal adaptational consequences under new situations.

Thus, in our particular case, the fusion of monastic and knightly roles in collectivistic frontier communities represented the emergence of innovative functions, while the dilemmas in which the king, clergy, and the knightly class were caught expressed a growing institutional lag. The political functions of the religio-military orders were related to the security and survival of their society in its new environment. Their ideals were culturally rooted and, to a degree, socially congruent. But the congruence of their innovations with the previously separated monastic and knightly roles did not imply congruence with the entrenched stratification system and political institutions. The latter, on the other hand, in spite of their growing disfunctionality, were also culturally rooted and institutionally supported. Thus a conflict developed between culturally rooted and functional *ideals*, and an institutionally supported but disfunctional *stratification system*. This, by the way, brings into sharp relief the repeated ideological assumption about the necessary connection between existing power-status positions and adequate social leadership.

Again, this innovative function may be viewed as a counter-change to basic changes in inter-societal relations through a redefinition of conventional roles. We have illustrated it by reference to the emergence of vassalage and feudalism as an innovative function, i.e. as an alternative to anarchy in the European situation. Later we have seen that feudalism itself, when transplanted to a significantly different inter-societal environment, entered a state of institutional lag. But inter-societal relations do not determine directly the form and content of innovative functions. One can only observe that factors from the inter-societal system are first internalized (i.e., perceived and integrated) by responding individuals and groups, and then translated, so to speak, into their own cultural terms, and finally become externalized (i.e. behaviorally reacted to and projected) into transformed institutions. This explains the relative success of the Jerusalemite innovations in social organization. It shows that adaptational forces are not simply functions related to survival, but that they vary with particular cultural identities which societies strive to preserve. This they do with no less determination (perhaps more) than that of mere self-preservation. By the same token, as one shifts attention to the remarkable process of feudal legislation in the Kingdom of Jerusalem, that consistent effort to confirm feudal customs and systematize them in writing, shielding the knightly class and vassalage against any threat from the state, one cannot escape the conclusion that self-conscious conservatism goes hand in hand with frightened non-functional elites.[22] Thus the same institutional lag which suggested the innovative functions of the religio-military orders, whose activities prolonged the existence of the Kingdom, also sustained the corollary built-in resistance to change. Ultimately, the result was a gradual detachment from reality which contributed most to the decline and fall of the Kingdom.

In conclusion, the above analysis seems to provide sub-

[22] On the peculiarity of feudal legislation in Jerusalem the French historian F. L. Ganshof, *Feudalism* (Harper, 1961), pp. 65-66, had this to say: "In the eastern states, however, it was feudalism with a difference. The feudalism of the Crusader states was something that has been aptly described as 'colonial' for it was created within a political framework set up by an army of lords and vassals, which constituted a species of military 'command' particularly exposed to attack. It is therefore not surprising that it should have exhibited well-marked peculiarities of its own. The system of feudal relationships was generalized and codified to a degree never known in the west, and much stronger emphasis was laid on the rights and prerogatives of vassals. The texts which deal with the feudalism of the Latin states, and in particular the collection known as the Assizes of Jerusalem, do not therefore throw much light on feudal institutions as they existed in Western Europe."

CHAPTER 3

stantial support for what has been suggested in the introduction of this study, namely, to the hypothesis of the inter-societal system. We have said that "If cultural diffusion represents a way by which societies present solutions of problems to one another (e.g. a tool, a technique, an idea) there is also the parallel phenomenon of societies introducing problems into one another's system. When viewed as interlocked political units impinging upon one another, any internal change in one system (economic, technological, military, ideological, etc.) which has a balance changing significance for a coexisting system, might induce countervailing efforts in the latter. This indirect influence (as distinguished from direct interpenetration by cultural diffusion or forceful intrusion) represents the role played by coexisting societies in the structure of one another. Thus if they become participants in an inter-societal system, they must orient their institutions to one another" (see above, p. 7).

It will be our task in the next analytical chapter to elaborate on the hypothesis of the inter-societal system and its induced functions, after we have described the core history of the Kingdom of Jerusalem.

The Critical Turning Points

Reasons for Encirclement and Isolation of the Latins

Chronologically we now arrive at the core of the Kingdom's history, leaving behind the opening acts of its historical drama. The kingships of Fulk, Baldwin III, and Amalric (1131-1174) marked a reluctant and inconsistent recognition on the part of the Franks of their inability to carry on the tremendous project of destroying Islamic power as far as Iraq and Egypt, while doing enough to provoke the Moslems into forming a power capable of destroying Jerusalem. With the unfolding of Frankish ambitions, the way was paved for ambitious empire builders on the Moslem side.

By their very presence, but more so by their policies and actions, the Franks provided the cement for the welding together of small Syrian emirates, first in defensive and then in offensive Jihads. The images of Imad-ad-Din Zangi and his son Nur-ad-Din Mahmud were formed in an atmosphere of common anxieties and hero-cravings throughout Syria, which facilitated the suppression of local particularism. Thus the political, religious, educational, and welfare renascence achieved by Nur-ad-Din in a unified Syria were expanded and crowned by the empire of Salah-ad-Din from Cairo to Mosul. In contradistinction, the foreign policy of the Franks was basically isolationistic and unimaginative. First, they failed to recognize and utilize Byzantine claims and interests in northern Syria. Instead of relinquishing Antioch to Byzantium (as agreed at the outset of the First Crusade, and as Emperors John and Manuel

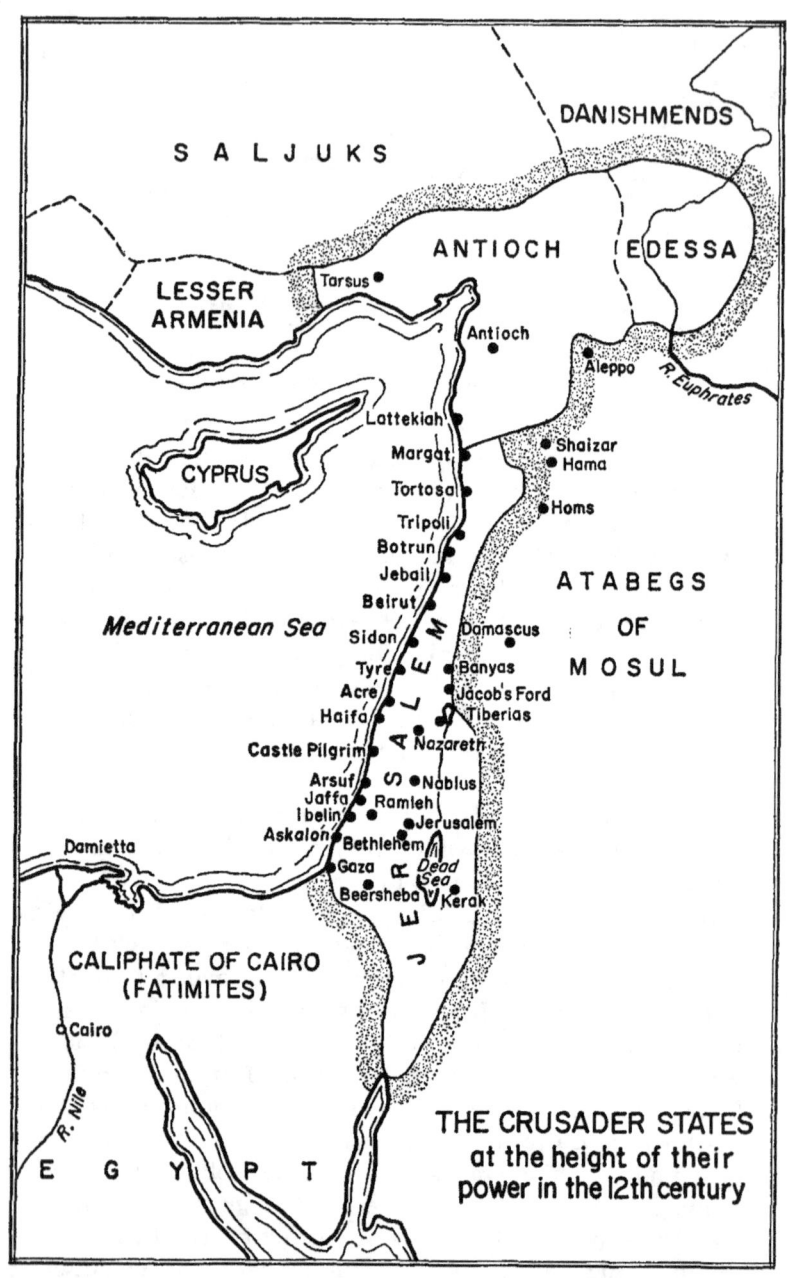

Map II: Crusader States at the Height of Their Power
Adapted from Edith Simon, *The Piebald Standard*
(Little, Brown, 1959).

aspired to in 1137, 1142, and 1159), thus committing a valuable ally to take the brunt of attacks along the Aleppo-Mosul axis, the Franks ignorantly posed in northern Syria as a multiple threat to Byzantine territory in Cilicia as well as to all Saljuqid states of Syria. Moreover, the effective alliance of Jerusalem and Damascus (1139-1147) against the expansion of Zangi into southern Syria was later betrayed by the Franks in their abortive attacks on Damascus, which liquidated the independence of a valuable buffer state and pushed it into the hands of Nur-ad-Din. This double isolationism not only relieved Zangi and his successor Nur-ad-Din from a formidable Byzantine "second front" in the north, but also removed the last barrier to Jerusalem in the south. Finally, the conquest of Egypt by the generals of Nur-ad-Din was made possible by Frankish inability to assure the Egyptians of their good intentions and maintain their defensive alliance with them. Instead, the Franks entertained the fantastic idea of conquering their ally. It is highly unrealistic to suppose that Amalric's greedy adventures in Egypt stood a chance of a lasting occupation, considering his meager resources in manpower, and the exposure of his northern rear, not to mention the inevitable resentment of Egyptian Moslems to Frankish rule. Even the Byzantines, with whom diplomatic ties at this stage were much improved, remained ambivalent to the prospect of Frankish control of Egypt. Their past experience with Normans and Franks in northern Syria was not conducive to a full-fledged and trustful cooperation. Yet an engagement of Nur-ad-Din's forces by Emperor Manuel in 1164-1169, or even Amalric's concurrence with the plan of a combined Franco-Byzantine offensive against Egypt in 1168, could make all the difference between success and failure for the Franks in Egypt.

Thus it may be concluded that if on the various frontiers with Moslem principalities the Franks gave the impression of attempting to devour everyone without having the capacity to do so, in their treatment of special alliances, such as those with Damascus and Egypt, they attempted to

CHAPTER 4

have their cake and eat it too, while in their Byzantine policy they wanted to get something for nothing and were reciprocated accordingly at their most critical moment. Both encirclement and isolation in the international system became the inevitable results of the above.

Let us now take a closer look at the international situation of the Franks, as leadership roles passed to the second generation of native crusaders. One historian characterized it in the following words: "The men of the first generation regarded all Moslem Syria as an unoccupied promised land. Their successors viewed the Moslems as joint occupants with themselves. The country which was theirs 'by divine right' was practically co-extensive with the land they now occupied. They discovered that their neighbours had much in common with themselves. They adopted Eastern dress and Eastern habits and ceased to be 'exiles' in a foreign land. The purpose of the first crusade was accomplished and its force was spent."[1] However, a stable *modus vivendi* with the adjacent Arab emirates of Syria was hardly acceptable even to leaders of the second and third generation Franks, such as Baldwin III and Amalric. As we shall see later, the problem of accommodation eventually divided the Franks into two parties, one favoring coexistence and expedient cooperation with available Moslem allies, and one pressing for uncompromising expansionism. Generally speaking, it was typical of fanatical newcomers from the west to take the adventurous point of view, while the more experienced and realistic lords of the east inclined towards moderation and prudence. Still, the major political developments showed that such potential allies as the Shiite population of Aleppo, the organized sect of the Ismailians (Assassins), the small but strategically valuable principality of Shaizar, and the independent and formidable kingdom of Damascus were all ultimately confronted with the choice between intolerant and abusive Christian lords and the Saljuqid champions of Islam. Only by honoring the wish of Syrian Arabs to re-

[1] W. B. Stevenson, *The Crusaders in the East* (Cambridge University Press, 1907), p. 146.

main politically free of any imperial pressure could the Franks establish a united front with them against encroachments from Iraq or Anatolia. We can now turn to a more systematic survey of major developments and turning points in the international system.

The Damascus-Jerusalem Alliance and the Containment of Zangi

In the summer of 1140, the armies of Jerusalem and Damascus united against a mighty enemy from the north. This was a result of diplomatic negotiations, the common purpose of which was to preserve the independence of Damascus. It was promptly achieved with great political and military benefits for the allies. The three key figures involved in this dramatic encounter were the Atabeg Imad-ad-Din Zangi of Mosul, the Wazir Muin-ad-Din Unur of Damascus, and King Fulk of Jerusalem. The developments which led to this important turning point will be better understood if Zangi's career is examined first.

Zangi was the son of a distinguished Saljuqid prince in the armies of Sultan Malik Shah, who was rewarded with the emirate of Aleppo in 1086, but lost it just before the advent of the First Crusade. When his father died in the civil wars over the Sultanate (1094), Zangi was ten years old, and he was taken to Mosul to be trained under the guardianship of his father's friend. In 1110 he participated in the first campaigns of Maudud against the Latins, conducted under the name of Jihads and authorized by the caliph of Bagdad. In 1113 he was the hero of the siege of Tiberias during the unsuccessful invasion of the Kingdom of Jerusalem by Maudud. The following year, he became a General under the new ruler of Mosul, Aksungur al-Bursuki. It was during this period that Zangi learned the strategies of stretching an arm to power struggles in Bagdad while setting a foothold in Aleppo and the whole of Syria as a base sufficiently remote from the capital of Saljuqid power. This pattern was set by al-Bursuki of Mosul and gave Zangi his opportunities for prominence. During the

CHAPTER 4

following years he was given one promotion after another in Iraq. His decisive aid to Sultan Mahmud in his power contests with the caliph (1125–1126) brought him the post of Military Governor of Bagdad and Iraq. In 1127 he was appointed atabeg for the sultan's son Alp Arslan in Mosul, from which he started his autonomous political career. "No position could have attracted Zangi more. In Bagdad he was overshadowed by the sultan. In Mosul he was already known and esteemed, and nowhere had he less to learn of the policy which the situation demanded."[2]

What were the policies which the situation in Mosul demanded? From the perspective of Mosul an ambitious ruler could look both to the center of Saljuqid domains and to their frontiers. Any change in Bagdad could have a direct impact upon Mosul's rulers and this made them a party to civil wars in Iraq, with aspirations for ultimate power in the capital not excluded. On the other hand, the Frankish threat to Aleppo in Syria, which was of much concern to Mosul, made it available as a protectorate for a greater power. Thus to an imaginative ruler of Mosul the possession of Aleppo could serve two complementary purposes: 1) it would reinforce the independence of Mosul in case of a rift with Bagdad; 2) with the role of defender of Islam against the Franks, Mosul could claim legitimate power over the Arab principalities in the Syrian frontier and eventually even in Bagdad itself. In either case, Mosul would become a great center of power in its own right. In this way a troublesome frontier coupled with political fragmentation in the interior availed Zangi of an expanding self-image vis-à-vis all Moslem and Frankish neighbours. His actions showed that he considered his prospective domination over Syria a precondition for a final attack upon the Franks.

Zangi acted swiftly and relentlessly. During 1127, the year of his accession to power, he consolidated his position around Mosul by obtaining (temporarily) the submission of the rival Ortuqid Turcomans. The strongholds of Nisi-

[2] *Ibid.*, p. 123.

bin, Sinjar, and Harran were annexed. The following year he advanced on Aleppo, seizing the connecting links of Manbij and Buza'a on his way, while his rear was made secure by a truce with Joscelin of Edessa. Aleppo welcomed his occupation as a protection against the Franks. But Zangi turned south against the dependencies of Damascus, Hamma, and Homs. He used the opportunity of the death of Tugtakin of Damascus to offer his successor, Taj al-Muluk Buri, a common front against the Franks. It was mainly a ruse on the part of Zangi to capture Hamma, a fact made dramatically evident to the Damascenes by the arrest of Buri's son, Sevinj, who came to negotiate in Aleppo. However, Damascus had just been attacked by Jerusalem from the south in 1129 and could only defend itself passively. Meanwhile, Zangi was forced to return to Bagdad to contest the Arab prince, Dubais ibn Sadaka, for the appointment over Syria. Zangi won and returned to Syria with an official diploma from the sultan. In 1130 he invaded Antioch (whose prince had been killed earlier that year in a war with the Danishmend Turks), but soon signed a truce. Between 1131 and 1134, Zangi took part in a civil war between the Caliph al-Mustarshid and Sultan Masud, and fought a war with the Kurds. All this time his military policies in Syria were pursued by his deputy Sawar. This gave the Franks a relative respite and the Damascenes an opportunity to recapture Hamma. In 1135 the emir of Damascus, Shams al-Muluk Ismail, was assassinated and succeeded by his brother, Shihab-ad-Din Mahmud. This seemed to Zangi an opportune moment to attack Damascus itself. But the real ruler of Damascus, a mamluk (formerly slave) general by the name of Muin ad-Din Unur, defended it effectively. Zangi then turned to a major invasion of Antioch, conquering a chain of fortresses on its eastern frontier between Aleppo and Hamma. The Arab city of Shaizar further south thereby became a dependency, and the Franks were pushed westwards toward the Orontes River. By the end of that year (1135) Zangi was back in Iraq again making another bid for power there

CHAPTER 4

as a protector of the new caliph, ar-Rashid. He switched sides midway, and emerged on the winning side of Sultan Masud. In 1137 Zangi renewed his offensive in Syria, still in the direction of Damascus. He failed to conquer Homs which was rigorously defended by Unur, but soon afterward scored a gain over King Fulk at Baarin in Tripoli. Fulk surrendered the fortress to Zangi in exchange for his release from the siege. At this juncture came the abortive Byzantine invasion of northern Syria (below, pp. 89-92) which interrupted everything. Zangi successfully evaded any showdown with Emperor John, but kept his own in Aleppo. After the Greeks' retreat in 1138 Zangi made a treaty with Damascus by which he received Homs in exchange for Baarin, married Shihab-ad-Din's mother and gave him his daughter to seal the "friendship." His goal remained, however, the conquest of Damascus—diplomatically if possible. His hands were now free to recapture the losses from the Greek invasion and to fight the Ortuqs near Mosul. The following year (1139) brought a number of unpredictable events. Shihab-ad-Din Mahmud of Damascus was assassinated and his brother Jamal-ad-Din Muhammad became the nominal emir. Zangi saw this as a good opportunity to make his final forceful claim, but Unur, now a personal enemy of Zangi, was again prepared for an undaunted stand. Thus, while Zangi was conquering Baalbek to the north of Damascus, Unur sent a special messenger to Jerusalem to negotiate a treaty.

It was Usamah ibn Munkid of Shaizar, a refugee prince and a former officer of Zangi, who tried to reach an agreement with the Franks on behalf of Unur. Similar attempts at negotiation had been unsuccessful in 1133 and 1138, but this time the Franks were attracted. The resulting treaty arranged for the following: Jerusalem's army would join Damascus in repelling the Zangi threat; Damascus would cover the cost of Jerusalem's forces with 20,000 pieces of gold a month; Banyas would be handed over to the Franks after its capture from Zangi's emir; hostages would be given to Jerusalem. The common interests of Jerusalem and Damascus were thus translated into action, and King Fulk promptly took his army north.

Jerusalem's intervention was decisive. Zangi could not withstand the combined forces of the two allied armies and abandoned his siege of Damascus. He retreated to Baalbek, leaving Banyas unprotected. Franks and Damascenes, fighting shoulder to shoulder in their siege of Banyas, forced its surrender to Unur, who turned it over to the Franks according to the agreement. Zangi plundered the environs of Damascus and retired in disgust to Mosul. He never returned to Syria again, although he still had six more years to live and a major victory over Edessa before him. Meanwhile, Unur paid a friendly visit to King Fulk, and was given a magnificent royal reception.

It is hard to say whether the containment of Zangi was a result of his own recklessness in forcing the issue of Moslem solidarity, or a reflection of a real possibility of a Franco-Syrian *modus vivendi*. It was up to the Franks, at this historical juncture, to choose between a "southern policy" which allowed for a lasting cooperation with Syrian principalities, and a "northern policy" of an expanding frontier. The latter alternative would act in the future as a catalyst to Islamic unification; its impact would resemble that of a foreign body in a large organism, alerting dormant-defensive "anti-bodies" to liquidate the intruder. The Franks, as we shall presently see, were divided on this problem as well as the Byzantine problem. If the actions of Baldwin II (1118-1131) had reflected a clear cut aim of occupying Aleppo and Damascus, Fulk's strategies (1131-1143) tended to the alternatives of *modus vivendi*. His main weakness, however, was a lack of determination in imposing upon the northern Franks the necessary cooperation with Byzantium which would have been consistent with his southern policy.

The Alienation of Byzantium and the Fall of Edessa

Fulk of Anjou became King of Jerusalem by marrying Melisende, the half-Armenian daughter of Baldwin II (who died without sons). Fulk's leadership was prearranged by the barons of Jerusalem. He was known as an experienced prince in Europe, a pilgrim to Jerusalem (1120), and later as an associate member of the Order of the Temple. In 1127 he was formally invited to marry Melisende with a view toward guaranteeing a male successor to Baldwin II. His crowning, together with his wife's, required an election by all direct vassals of the Kingdom who were represented in the feudal *Haute Cour*. However, much depended upon the actual alignments of military power, especially in contested and doubtful cases. Despite his baronial backing, Fulk's accession to the throne (1131) was associated with two feudal rebellions.

Fulk's first problem was with the principalities of the north, namely with Alice of Antioch (his wife's sister) and with Pons of Tripoli, who made it quite clear that they had no intention of recognizing him as overlord. Alice, who occupied the post of regent for her little daughter Constance (hereditary heiress to Bohemond II), had ambitious plans for Antioch and herself. She was supported mainly by the native Syrian and Greek population of the city, and had already attempted to defy her own father (Baldwin II) by seeking the aid of Zangi (1129). Fulk had participated in the suppression of that rebellion with the aid of the religio-military orders. After the death of the ruler of Edessa, Joscelin I, who had been regent of Antioch for Constance, Alice returned to power and made another attempt at emancipation from Jerusalem. Some of the barons of Antioch did not concur with her plans and summoned Fulk. Thus, immediately after his coronation Fulk led the army of Jerusalem northward to Antioch, where he met in battle the united forces of the two rebellious princes. His victory at Chastel Rouge, again due largely to the support of the Temple and Hospital, decided the questions of legitimacy.

Not long after this, Fulk had to handle another rebellion in his own kingdom, involving the Count of Jaffa, Hugh of Le Puiset, a lover of the Queen, now accused of treacherous plots. In the spirit of the time, Hugh was married to a rich, old widow whose possessions made him a still mightier baron, but his love remained with the young Queen. This brought him into conflicts with his sons-in-law (who were about his age). When matters reached the boiling point, Hugh went with his fighting force to the Moslems in nearby Askalon and secured their support against his king, whereupon the "allies" invaded the Kingdom. A dangerous situation ensued. While the royal army was marching on the barony of Jaffa, the Arabs of Damascus (Shams-al-Muluk, 1132) took advantage of this civil war to conquer the Frankish fortress of Banyas in the north. The rebellion was soon suppressed and Hugh was sentenced to exile.

Fortunately for the Franks, violent civil wars were in progress at the time in Iraq, Egypt, and Damascus. Zangi's general, Sawar, was active in northern Syria, however, and Fulk had to rush for aid. On his way to Antioch (1133) he saved Pons of Tripoli from encirclement by Turcoman troops in the Nosairi mountains, and reestablished feudal ties with him. The Queen's sister, Hodierna, was given in marriage to Pons' son, Raymond II, and Fulk's constable in Antioch married Pons' daughter. Sawar was attempting then to cut the communication links between Edessa and Antioch, but Fulk's successful intervention thwarted it. In 1135 came the major offensive of Zangi (described above) which ended in the conquest of the Antiochene frontier fortresses. Zangi had to return to Mosul, and Fulk was forced to return to Antioch, where another power was complicating developments there. Through some plots with Radulph, the new Latin patriarch, Alice was again in control of Antioch. She also had an imaginative plan to make Antioch a protectorate of Byzantium. Her idea was to have Emperor John's son, Manuel, marry her daughter, Constance, and thus become Prince of Antioch. Successful negotiations to that effect began in Constantinople. As one historian put it, "Her [Alice's] action may have been, as the horrified Crusaders declared, due to the caprice of her ambition; but in fact it offered the best solution for the preservation of northern Syria. The Greek element was strong

CHAPTER 4

in Antioch. The Moslem menace was growing under Zangi; and the Empire was the only power strong enough to check it. A vassal-state ruled under imperial suzerainty first by the half-Armenian Alice and then jointly by a Byzantine prince and a Frankish princess, might well have served to weld Greek and Frank together for the defense of Christendom."[3]

But Fulk and the Frank barons thought otherwise, and decided secretly to bring a thirty-nine-year-old prince from Europe and marry him immediately to the nine-year-old princess of Antioch. Their choice was Raymond of Poitiers, a younger son of Duke William IX of Aquitaine, whose daughter was married to Fulk's son. This act was designed to abolish the Byzantine orientation of Alice, and also to thwart Roger II of Sicily (a cousin of Bohemond II) whose Mediterranean plans included a continuation of the Norman dynasty in Antioch. The intrigue worked perfectly. A Knight of the Hospitallers served as a guide to Raymond in his dangerous trip, and the new anti-Byzantine ruler took possession of Antioch. The Latin patriarch Radulph was instrumental in consolidating Raymond's position, not without power ambitions of his own. But as soon as Raymond was established, he violated all previous agreements with the patriarch, and became sole ruler with the barons' support. Shortly afterwards (1136), he invaded Cilicia which was occupied by Armenian Roupenian princes. Before long, all the fronts in northern Syria were reopened. A Damascene force, with aid from the native Christians of Lebanon, captured and killed Count Pons of Tripoli, whereupon his successor, Raymond II, revenged by massacring thousands of his Christian villagers. Fulk of Jerusalem took his army again to the north. Meanwhile, Zangi was back in Syria pursuing his project of creating an empire by attacking Arab cities which refused to "unite" and by pushing the Franks westwards. In the midst of these military developments, both Moslems and Franks were surprised to

---

[3] S. Runciman, *History of the Crusades*, Vol. II (Cambridge University Press, 1957), p. 198.

learn of a powerful invasion of northern Syria by the Byzantine army under Emperor John (1137).

At the gates of Antioch, after a show of force, the Greek emperor requested and received the equivalent of feudal homage and submission from arrogant Raymond. Fulk stayed helpless and evasive in Jerusalem. He could no longer miss seeing that the Byzantine ambitions in Syria were balancing and countervailing the ambitions of Zangi. In his letter to Raymond he wrote: "We all know, and our elders have long taught us that Antioch was part of the Empire of Constantinople till it was taken from the Emperor by the Turks, who held it for fourteen years, and that the Emperor's claims about the treaties made by our ancestors [meaning the leaders of the First Crusade] are correct. Ought we then to deny the truth and oppose what is right?"[4] However, it was Fulk's own fault that the pro-Byzantine policy of Alice was sabotaged, and it was his opportunity now to negotiate a far-reaching agreement with Emperor John. Instead he left the initiative in the hands of Raymond of Antioch and Joscelin of Edessa who had no intention of respecting their oaths and faked ceremonies with the Byzantines. Meanwhile, Zangi concluded a quick truce with Damascus and began mobilizing help from all the Moslem world in the face of the Greek danger.

The interests of the Byzantine empire in Syria in the 12th century were basically defensive and had to do mainly with the general Turkish danger. Although its western frontiers were also quite turbulent and required intermittent war and diplomacy, the Byzantines were sufficiently informed about the Moslem world to realize that if the Abassid empire united again under one military leader as in the days of Alp Arslan, another disaster (like the one at Manzikert in 1071) was likely to bring the Turkish hosts to the gates of Constantinople. Most of central and eastern Anatolia was still occupied by two Turkish kingdoms, the Sultanate of Rum and the Danishmends. Farther east and south was Zangi of Mosul, a party to power struggles in Bagdad and a

[4] *Ibid.*, p. 213.

CHAPTER 4

ruler of territories in Syria, officially invested by the caliph with the Jihad against the Franks. A foothold in Syria would enable Byzantium to pursue more effectively the basic line of its traditional diplomacy in the east, namely, the prevention of the rise of any major power at its frontier. In the past, it was a matter of playing Cairo and Bagdad against one another. Now it was a matter of reducing and balancing Turkish kingdoms. A direct contact with Zangi meant a possibility to act in the rear of the Anatolian Turks. On the other hand, Zangi as a potential Sultan over Iraq and Syria was definitely a major threat to Byzantium. The Franks were an obstacle to Zangid ambitions in Syria, and as such they were considered a Byzantine asset. However, if the Franks were to succeed in establishing a large kingdom in the east, what applied to the Saljuqs would apply to them. Thus, the appearance of Emperor John before the gates of Antioch in 1137 was preceded by successful military campaigns in Anatolia and Cilicia, and was to be followed by action in Syria that would contain the expansion of Zangi while subordinating the Franks of Antioch to the frontier interests of Byzantium. Nothing could better insure the security of all Frankish principalities in the Levant, especially Edessa which was an obvious target of Zangi. Surprisingly, it was Joscelin II of Edessa who later played a major role in instigating anti-Greek riots in the streets of Antioch while the emperor was in the palace negotiating arrangements for a permanent Byzantine base in the city.

The Byzantine campaign in Syria (1138) proved unsuccessful. Having received the submission of Raymond, it was "agreed" that a combined Greco-Frankish offensive should be conducted in Syria, with Aleppo, Homs, Hama, and Shaizar as the major targets. If any of these major cities were conquered, Raymond was to move there and relinquish Antioch to the emperor, a condition which paralyzed genuine cooperation on the part of the Franks in advance. John, for his part, did not make a major effort to persist in his attack on Aleppo; after a brief siege, he moved to the independent Arab Munqidite principality of Shaizar. His avoidance of a showdown with the forces of Zangi may be explained either by mistrust of his reluctant Frankish allies, or by some diplomatic understanding with Zangi, or perhaps both. The ensuing siege of Shaizar was futile. Although the city was conquered, its special citadel withstood the powerful sieging machines of the Greeks. Finally, the emperor returned to Antioch, taking with him monetary compensation and gifts from the emir of Shaizar, Abu'l Asakir Sultan. Thus, except for the reconquest of the eastern fortresses on the frontier with Aleppo, nothing was changed. But John, who was a tough warrior and a wise strategist, intended to try again if he could work out a reliable understanding with his "allies." Raymond and Joscelin, however, felt free now to renounce their allegiance except for a symbolic tribute, and they frightened the emperor out of Antioch. The Greek army retreated to Cilicia, but not without the hope of a forceful return.

All this time Fulk was maintaining his stand of nonintervention. His actions in the following years reflected an almost complete disengagement from northern Syrian affairs. In 1139-1140 Emperor John was busy in Anatolia against Mohammed, the Danishmend emir, while Zangi recovered his losses from Antioch and began his last offensive against Damascus. This activated the Damascus-Jerusalem alliance which defeated Zangi (described above). Fulk now turned his full attention to fortification and castle building in the Kingdom of Jerusalem (1140-1143). As early as 1136 a strong fortress was built on the frontier with Askalon at Beit-Gibrin and entrusted to the Hospitallers, while the Templars built a fortress in Gaza. Soon many strongholds were added to the south. First were Ibelin (Yabne) and Blanchegarde (Tel-as-Safiya), built to the north and east of Askalon. Then the important fortress of Kerak of Moab was constructed east of the Dead Sea to supplement Montreal (Shaubak) and Ailat. In 1142 the Hospitallers settled in the principality of Tripoli, occupying the great frontier fortress of Hisn-al-Akrad (Kerak de chevaliers) and Rafania, which guarded the approaches to the Bukaia

CHAPTER 4

Valley, the main entrance to the seashore. Raymond II of Tripoli was so desperate that he signed an agreement with the Hospitallers not to make any treaties with the Moslems without their consent. The southern policy of Fulk was thus firmly established.

The year 1141, however, reopened the Byzantine problem. The death of Mohammed the Danishmend enabled Emperor John to return to Cilicia and settle his accounts with the Franks. First he moved against Joscelin at Tell Bashir and reduced him to full submission. Then he advanced on Raymond. This time the lines were clearly drawn. John demanded an unconditional surrender and full control of Antioch. His plan was to install his son Manuel over Isouria, Cilicia, and northern Syria. Raymond replied that he was ruling Antioch only as the husband of Constance and, therefore, had no legitimate power to transfer the principality. The barons, he said, would rebel even if the princess herself would consent. And last but not least, the Latin patriarch was not prepared to be replaced by a Greek patriarch. The matter, then, was to be decided by war. It was close to winter and John, after devastating the countryside, retired to Cilicia to prepare for his coming siege of Antioch. He wrote to Fulk asking for permission to visit Jerusalem with his army; the King agreed, with the polite suggestion that the emperor come unaccompanied by military forces. It is remarkable that Fulk, who had indicated a good grasp of balance-of-power politics in his recent anti-Zangid alliance with Damascus, neglected this last opportunity to install the Byzantines in Antioch as a northern complementary balance to the Zangid empire.

Presently events took an unexpected turn. John died suddenly in April 1143 in an accident during a wild boar hunt, and his successor Manuel hurried to Constantinople to insure his new rule. Raymond of Antioch took the offensive and invaded Cilicia, but was soon driven out by the generals of Manuel, who pursued him to the walls of Antioch. Manuel forced him to go in person to Constantinople, humiliate himself there on the grave of John, and take an oath as a reduced vassal. Meanwhile, King Fulk also died, in a pleasure hunt near Acre (1143), and his wife Melisende took over the affairs of Jerusalem. As for Joscelin of Edessa, he was busy making treaties with Sawar (Zangi's governor of Aleppo) against Antioch, and with Ortuquid princes.

At this juncture, Zangi felt free to strike a major blow. Edessa was practically isolated, and no one was likely to make a move to aid Joscelin. He made a surprise attack while Joscelin was away, and conquered Edessa. The three bishops who defended the city (the Latin Hugh, the Jacobite Basil, and the Armenian John) held the besiegers for four weeks but had to surrender on Christmas Eve (December 24, 1144), whereupon a slaughter of all the Latins took place (the native Christians were spared). For destroying this Frankish principality, Zangi won the title "victorious king" from the caliph. Until then, Zangi had been nominally just an atabeg to the sultan's son Alp Anslan in Mosul; now he became a fully recognized and legitimate king. And, not less significantly, his communication lines with Syria were greatly improved, the eastern bank of the Euphrates was soon cleared of Franks, and the establishment of a strong Zangid empire was in full progress.

Raymond of Antioch, who was not on friendly terms with Joscelin, was probably too weak to interfere anyway, as a result of his recent war with the Greeks (also, he may have been in Constantinople at the time), while Melisende's forces were too far to reach Edessa in time. Thus, it is quite clear that the fall of Edessa was a direct consequence of the alienation of Byzantium.

From the Second Crusade to the Unification of Moslem Syria

Two men played central roles in the developments which led to the unification of Islamic Syria and the precarious isolation of the Kingdom of Jerusalem: Nur-ad-Din Mahmud and Baldwin III. Their rivalry evolved mainly around Damascus, which was the point of balance of the Syrian

CHAPTER 4

system, but there was also a "second front" in the north, around Antioch, strategically so situated that it could easily become the Achilles' heel of either party in the south. Thus it was necessary to have a well-coordinated long-range policy on two interdependent fronts. If unity of purpose and effort is considered decisive, then Nur-ad-Din, whose domain lay between northern and southern Franks, had the advantage of a single centralized control with shorter and inner communication lines. But Nur-ad-Din could not move in full force in one direction without dangerously exposing his rear. Precisely this was the advantage of the Franks: their rears both north and south could have been left unthreatened while concentrating effort upon Nur-ad-Din.[5] But they lacked the necessary integration of purpose and overall comprehension of the requirements of the situation. Thus, they dissipated their energies in courageous but foolhardy acts which played directly into the hands of Nur-ad-Din.

A comparison of their respective ages at the death of Zangi (Nur-ad-Din 30, Baldwin 16) gives only a partial clue to their differences. It was after all a conflict between forces much greater than two personalities. The stage, as set by their respective fathers (Zangi and Fulk), gave each of the successive rivals an equal chance to influence Syrian affairs. In fact, the initiative was still in the hands of Jerusalem (despite the fall of Edessa) if one considers the existing Damascus-Jerusalem alliance. Yet, it was Nur-ad-Din who emerged as the greater statesman, both in his foreign policy and inner social organization. We shall concentrate here on the international wills, policies, and forces, and leave the social structure to another chapter.

Taking as points of departure the fall of Edessa (1144) and the murder of Zangi (1146), the picture may be best understood if we follow the movements of major initiatives taken and reacted to, held or lost, by the various rivals.

The Franks were so alarmed by their setbacks in the north that they issued desperate calls for help to their European kinsmen, thus initiating the response known as the Second

[5] See Map I, p. 21.

Crusade. It was destined not only to reinforce Byzantine distrust of the Syrian Franks, but also to play a major role in the disastrous alienation of Damascus from Jerusalem. It would have been much better if Europe had just sent a few thousand "volunteers" to the ranks of the religio-military orders (whose effectiveness was well known by then) while allowing Byzantium to play her natural role in northern Syria.[6] As it was, Emperor Manuel was bound to become antagonistic toward the advance of Louis VII of France and Conrad of Germany to the Levant. It could liberate Raymond of Antioch from his recent dependency upon Constantinople, or even renew Frankish encroachments on the eastern frontier of Byzantium. Since the empire was preparing for another war with the Normans of Sicily, and the European kings behaved quite belligerently while passing through Constantinople, it seemed reasonable to Manuel to accept a truce offered by Sultan Mas'ud of Anatolia (1147). This, of course, accounts for the ensuing destruction of the bulk of the crusading armies in Asia Minor. But they finally managed to reach Syria by sea, and in sufficient numbers to engage in an abortive attack upon Damascus (1148). For this latter act against an ally, chief responsibility lay with the leaders of Jerusalem.

Upon the death of Zangi, every one of the affected parties moved in a reasonable direction except Jerusalem, which was then ruled by Fulk's widow Melisende and her young son Baldwin. Zangi's eldest son, Saif-ad-Din, went to assume power in Mosul, while Nur-ad-Din hurried to Aleppo. Unur of Damascus moved northward and recaptured Baalbek, Hamma, and Homs. Raymond of Antioch attacked Aleppo from the west, while Joscelin returned to Edessa, besieging its citadel. Similarly the Ortuqids invaded the Zangid realm in the northeast. The first known act of Jerusalem at this juncture was violation of its treaty with Damascus in Transjordan.

[6] Ironically, it was St. Bernard, who had a high esteem for the Orders and much contempt for secular knighthood, who played a central role in inspiring the Second Crusade of regular armies.

CHAPTER 4

Nur-ad-Din held his own in Aleppo, and went immediately to Edessa to repel Joscelin's attack. This was also calculated to forestall his brother in Mosul. In suppressing the Christian uprising in Edessa, Nur-ad-Din used an iron hand. Armenians and Jacobites were massacred by the thousands, and the rest of the native Christians became refugees. He then made an agreement with Saif-ad-Din by which their father's realm was divided into eastern and western parts with Mosul and Aleppo as capitals. Both brothers had their hands full with invading enemies, and could not afford a war of succession. This partition deprived Nur-ad-Din of the military resources of Mosul, but it also freed him from involvements with Ortoks, Kurds, sultan, and caliph in Iraq. Moreover, he could now become more acceptable as an equal ally to Syrian emirs, and he was determined to make the most of it. In March 1147 he reached an agreement with Unur of Damascus, married his daughter, received Hamma back, and promised to respect the independence of Damascus. For Unur, however, Jerusalem remained a valuable ally against a possible breach with Aleppo.

At this point Unur learned of the rebellion of one of his officers in the Jaulan and the movement of the Frankish army toward the fortresses of Bosra and Artah. He had no choice but to turn to Nur-ad-Din, who was delighted to offer aid; and the Moslem allies reached the disputed fortress before the Franks. As Baldwin was bravely leading the retreat (which was his first military performance) messengers from Unur came to offer provisions and to assure Baldwin's safety. Thus Damascus persisted in its loyalty to the alliance with Jerusalem even after the attack of the Second Crusade and after the death of Unur, as evidenced by their refusal to participate in Nur-ad-Din's offensives in the south (1150), in their avoidance of the brief Ortuqid invasion of Jerusalem (1152), and in Mujir-ad-Din's offer of Baalbek to Jerusalem in return for a common defense of Damascus (1154) (see below, pp. 101-106).

Secure in his southern rear, Nur-ad-Din could now join in the attacks of the Sultan Mas'ud upon Antioch as a result of his peace with Manuel. During 1147-1148 Nur-ad-Din captured most of the Antioch territory beyond the Orontes. But these operations stopped at the end of the summer of 1147, when news of the advancing Second Crusade came. Nur-ad-Din's reaction was to call upon his brother in Mosul for aid against any eventuality. In his wildest dreams he could not have foreseen the attack on Damascus.

At the major council of kings and princes, barons and clergy and the Masters of the Orders at Acre in June 1148, Damascus was chosen as a target of conquest. In vain were the desperate appeals of Raymond of Antioch for help in attacking Nur-ad-Din at Aleppo. Similarly, the original stimulus of the Second Crusade, namely Edessa, was ignored. Was the decision a reflection of Louis' and Conrad's disinclination to interfere in a Byzantine sphere of influence, or were they only following the guidance of the local Franks? If so, why would the leaders of Jerusalem press for an attack on an ally whose value they knew from the days of Zangi and Fulk? It was clear that the combined armies of the two Zangids would come to help Unur, while the latter was certain not to interfere in the north. Again, if it was indeed a policy inaugurated by the Jerusalemite lords, how can it be explained that they were later accused of plotting with Unur in the besieged city and causing the retreat of the entire expedition after five days? Were the Jerusalemites divided into two opposing parties on this matter? Did the Europeans wish to install a prince of their ranks in Damascus rather than leaving it to the Kingdom of Jerusalem? Such questions can only receive conjectural answers, but one thing is certain: "Operation Damascus" had an abundance of leaders and a lack of leadership.[7]

[7] Stevenson (*ibid.*, p. 160) does not accept the versions which follow William of Tyre's account, concerning the movement of the armies from the southwest side of the city with orchards to the southeast side with no water and food. He points out that experienced warriors cannot be persuaded to make such moves without checking these facilities. He also emphasizes that Moslem historians do not mention this move at

CHAPTER 4

Unur fully exploited the balancing pressure of Nur-ad-Din and Saif-ad-Din without yielding to their demand that the defense of the city be handed over to them. When the dust was settling upon the footsteps of the retreating crusaders, Damascus was still independent, but the seeds of a pro-Nur-ad-Din party were sown within it.

As for the Latin side, two epilogues rounded out their fiasco. The first was another plan to attack Askalon for which a gathering spot was fixed, but the army of Jerusalem never showed up; the crusaders dispersed without installing any new prince in the east. The second incident was more ominous. There was among the crusaders a Prince Bertram (grandson of Raymond from the First Crusade) who captured the fortress of al-Arima in the county of Tripoli with the intention of using it as a stepping stone to claim Tripoli for himself. The Tripolitanians had previously poisoned his father Alfonso (at the outset of the Second Crusade) for the same reason. Raymond II of Tripoli called upon Unur for military help. The latter invited Nur-ad-Din and they both razed and sacked the castle, taking Bertram prisoner, with the approval of Raymond and his mother-in-law Queen Melisende of Jerusalem.

Now Nur-ad-Din was prepared to take the initiative. During the next decade a chain of events occurred which transformed him from the Prince of Aleppo to the King of all Arab Syria, dwarfing all other rulers, including his brother in Mosul, King Baldwin III, even Emperor Manuel. Indeed, his military achievements might be credited to the talents of his excellent generals, Shirkuh the Kurd and Ibn-ad-Daya, a capable and learned administrator. Also, the immigration of Turcoman tribes into Syria provided him with much-needed manpower (up to 10,000 horsemen) eager

---

all. His explanation is that the siege was removed simply when it became clear that it had no chance of succeeding without a prolonged effort. This shows how decisive was the balancing force of Nur-ad-Din. It is quite possible that the local Franks changed their minds during the siege, as they pondered the danger of cooperation between Damascus and Nur-ad-Din.

to fight. But his main strength lay in the institutional reforms which he initiated in Syria and which he inspired by personal example. As one historian put it: "In contrast to his father, Zangi, he had by his life and conduct laid the foundation for that moral unification of Moslem forces on which alone a real political and military unity could be reared."[8] That is why the Arabs of Syria only feared Zangi ("the victorious king") but gradually learned to support his son Nur-ad-Din ("the just king") in spite of ethnical differences between the Saljuqid ruling class of warriors and the local Arab population.

Although Jerusalem seemed to have restored diplomatic relations with Damascus quickly, as shown by their new treaty of May 1149, they did not tie Unur's hands with respect to cooperation with Nur-ad-Din. Thus, Unur was compelled to send detachments to Nur-ad-Din's army which was engaged in Antioch. There Raymond was acting together with a new ally, the Assassins of Masyaf under Ali ibn Wafa. The reinforced armies of Nur-ad-Din defeated them severely (June 1149) and killed both Raymond and ibn Wafa in the battle of Inab (again the head of the prince of Antioch was sent to the caliph of Bagdad in a silver case), while Baldwin, whose actions were clearly not coordinated with Raymond, came a few days later only to halt the offensive at the gates of Antioch. Had the Franks been united under one authority, their full potential and initiative could have defeated Nur-ad-Din in this second front which, strategically speaking, was a Frankish asset. Next year Baldwin had to hurry north again, when Turcoman forces captured Joscelin of Tell Bashir and sent him as a prisoner to Aleppo. Antioch had not suffered a greater defeat since the days of the *ager sanguinis* ("field of blood"). Then it had been a result of Aleppo's refusal to become an oppressed protectorate of Antioch, and it showed Damascus' willingness to aid Aleppo when not ruled from

[8] H.A.R. Gibb, "The Life of Nur-ad-Din," in Setton and Baldwin (eds.), *A History of the Crusades*, Vol. II (University of Pennsylvania Press, 1960), p. 527.

CHAPTER 4

Mosul. Now the refusal of Damascus to become an oppressed protectorate of Jerusalem, coupled with the renewed independence of Aleppo from Mosul, enabled Nur-ad-Din to crush the power of Antioch with an all-Syrian coalition. Baldwin III found himself in a situation very similar to that which his grandfather, Baldwin II, had been in thirty years earlier, but with more adverse military and political conditions. Moslem Syria was growing stronger now independently of Iraq, more inclined to unity, and had great leadership of its own. Before long all of Antioch's territories beyond the Orontes River were conquered, while Sultan Mas'ud captured Marash and Duluk to the northeast. This was followed by the division of all the other Christian territories between the Orontes and the Euphrates among Nur-ad-Din, Mas'ud, and Timurtash the Ortuqid (Aintab and Duluk to Mas'ud; Tell Bashir and Ravendel to Nur-ad-Din; Samosata and Birejik to Timurtash). Thus victorious in the north, Nur-ad-Din felt encouraged to press more vigorously for the annexation of Damascus.

At the end of 1149 Unur of Damascus died, but Nur-ad-Din was compelled to rush to Mosul where his brother and ally Saif-ad-Din had also died. With the aid of Ortuqid princes, Nur-ad-Din reduced the successor brother, Qutb-ad-Din, to recognition of the status quo, and by 1150 he was back near Damascus demanding detachments for a joint attack with the Egyptian fleet on Jerusalem's coast. In Damascus the nominal ruler was Mujir-ad-Din Abak (Tugtakin's grandson), but power was as usual in the hands of the military. Mu'aiyid-ad-Din Ibn as-Sufi (the prefect) pleaded the treaty with Jerusalem and refused cooperation. Baldwin was prompt in moving his army to the aid of Damascus, and Nur-ad-Din gave up. Although popular opinion was rising in Damascus in favor of Nur-ad-Din, Baldwin's movements to northern Syria and to the aid of Damascus worried him. He was determined to annex Damascus and make it an active check on Baldwin in the south so that he could consolidate and safeguard his expansions in the north. By the summer of 1151 the treaty between Damascus and Jerusalem was about to expire and Nur-ad-Din made another attempt to take over Damascus. Again Baldwin moved his army to protect the independence of Damascus, and, exactly as in the days of Zangi, Nur-ad-Din had to retreat to Baalbek. Mujir-ad-Din permitted Frankish knights to visit the bazaars of his city for supplies while he went to Baldwin's camp for a friendly conference. Instead of pursuing Nur-ad-Din, the allies decided to make a combined expedition to Bosra in Transjordan to attack its rebellious emir who had cooperated with Nur-ad-Din. The lands of the Jaulan had been practically a condominium of Damascus and Jerusalem since the days of Tugtakin, and their income was divided accordingly. A short while after this expedition failed, the emir of Bosra began plotting with the Franks against Damascus. To counteract this, Mujir-ad-Din opened negotiations with Nur-ad-Din. In 1151 he visited Aleppo and made a treaty by which he was recognized as Nur-ad-Din's officer in Damascus. But he had no intention of abandoning Baldwin's help entirely. He disclaimed responsibility for Turcoman raids on Banyas (1151) and refused to join a Turcoman army from Mardin in a raid on Jerusalem (1152); he also continued to pay the monetary tribute to Baldwin.

Up to about this time Baldwin was not the exclusive King of Jerusalem; he shared his authority with his mother Melisende. She was supported by the able constable of the army, Manasses of Hierges, and the latter, through marriage with the Ibelin family of the south, aligned most of the southern nobility behind her. Territorially this coalition controlled the entire area of Jerusalem south of Galilee, while Baldwin's supporters were northerners, such as Humphrey of Toron and the religio-military orders, whose power was growing steadily. Baldwin had always been the recognized chief in warfare, but it is hard to say to what extent he influenced policy during his early years. In 1150, however, when he reached the age of 20, he and his party were prepared to fight a civil war to force his mother off the throne. By 1152, after some fighting and maneuvering,

CHAPTER 4

Baldwin subdued all opposition and was crowned King Baldwin III. In a short while, he had Jerusalem as his domain in addition to Acre, Tyre, and other domains in the north. All power and responsibility was now his, although not without consent of the High Court. He could shape a definite policy and execute it. What would he do?

The political horizons were ominous in the north. Antioch, which had shrunk to the western bank of the Orontes, was ruled temporarily by the Latin patriarch Aimery, and the key to a much-needed leadership lay in the future marriage of Constance. Emperor Manuel was interested (as his father John had been) in installing a Byzantine prince, while the local nobility was again trying to thwart this trend. In Tripoli Raymond II had been murdered at the gates of his city by assassins (1152), and Baldwin, who was there at the time, had arranged for the succession of a twelve-year-old child, Raymond III, with his mother Hodierna. A reinforcement of Templar Knights was installed in the fortress of Tortosa. Damascus was drifting into the hands of the pro-Nur-ad-Din party, and its vacillating generals and emir had been accused of treason. There was, however, one isolated spot in the southern frontier of Jerusalem which was vulnerable to attack, namely Askalon.

By the middle of the 12th century the decadence of the Fatimid caliphate in Cairo was so advanced and the chain of murderous intrigues so weakened its military capacity that it was well known in Jerusalem. Baldwin was swayed in the direction of least resistance, and led the entire forces of his realm to siege Askalon. All the great lords and bishops and the two Masters of the Orders were there. The Templars were particularly well represented (they had previously been installed in the fortress of Gaza for the encirclement of Askalon) and had much to say about the conduct of the siege and the division of booty. Heavy sieging machines and a tower were used, and even a small fleet of fifteen boats headed by Gerard of Sidon participated. The latter, however, were easily defeated by the Egyptian navy.

CRITICAL TURNING POINTS

Finally Askalon surrendered (August 1153) and was converted into a Latin stronghold with Amalric, the King's brother, as its lord. The Moslems were allowed to evacuate the city by agreement, and the riches of Askalon fell prey to the Latins.

All this time Nur-ad-Din made only one attempt to attack Banyas, together with the reluctant army of Damascus. Before they could do any damage to the exposed town, they had a quarrel and dispersed.

It appeared as if the good fortunes of Jerusalem lay in a southern orientation. To the extent that ties with Damascus could be strengthened and its role as a buffer state maintained, this seemed to be true. Mujir-ad-Din and his officers were leaning heavily on Baldwin's support (now offering him even larger sums of money), while the population was growing more and more resentful of the Frankish protectorate. "While Frankish lords journeyed and raided as they pleased over Damascene territory, Frankish ambassadors came to the city to collect the money for their king."[9] The emir of Baalbek, Ayub (Saladin's father), was organizing a plot with the restive leaders of Damascus, and the position of its ruler became precarious. The city longed for the return of "the just king," and a release from insecurity and humiliation.

Thus, during the winter after the conquest of Askalon, while Baldwin relaxed, having dispersed his troops to their various estates, Nur-ad-Din closed in on Damascus. As early as January 1154, his blockade of the city's grain supply from the north was causing havoc and distress, while his agents were sowing intrigues and intimidation within the walls. "The price of a sack of wheat," writes the contemporary Damascene chronicler, "reached twenty-five dinars and even more. A large number of persons withdrew from the town, ... it was said that Nur-al-Din was determined to proceed to the siege of Damascus and hoped to capture it by this means, since it was difficult for him to break down its resistance owing to the strength of its sultan and the

[9] Runciman, *ibid.*, p. 340.

number of its troops and auxiliaries."[10] The coming attack, then, could not have been a surprise to Baldwin. In the middle of April Nur-ad-Din moved with full force on Damascus, while Mujir-ad-Din sent a desperate call to Baldwin promising the city of Baalbek in return for succor. If Nur-ad-Din had had to depend only on his own forces the siege would have lasted for months and even the slow-moving Franks would have reached the field. But public opinion was already in favor of his entrance, and the city troops gave him little resistance. This is how the Damascene chronicler describes the conquest: "Owing to the bad management of the authorities and the foreordained decrees, there was not a breathing soul, either of troops or townsmen, upon the wall, save for a negligible handful of Turks, whose resistance could be discounted, on one of the towers. One of the footsoldiers went forward to the wall, upon which there was a Jewish woman, who let down a rope to him. He climbed up and obtained a footing on the wall, unperceived by any, and was followed by a number of others. Nur-al-Din's troops then hoisted a standard, and planting it on the wall shouted Ya Mansur (O victorious one), whereupon the troops and citizens ceased to make further resistance owing to the affection which they entertained for Nur-al-Din, and his justice and good reputation. One of the woodcutters hastened with his axe to the East Gate and broke its bolts; the gate was thrown open, and Nur-al-Din's askar [cavalry] entered by it with ease and confidence, and proceeded swiftly through the main streets. Not one man put up any resistance to their advance."[11] When Baldwin's army arrived it was all over; Nur-ad-Din had become the master of a unified Syria.

In order to fully understand the causes of this turning

[10] Ibn al-Qalanisi, *The Damascus Chronicle of the Crusades* (tr. by H.A.R. Gibbs) (Luzel & Co., 1932), p. 317.

[11] *Ibid.*, p. 319; see also further details of Nur-ad-Din's prohibition of plundering; appointment of Mujir-ad-Din to another city; and almost immediate organization of welfare services, reduction of duties, and retainment of the existing civic authorities.

point in the balance of power let us return to the Damascene chronicler in his description of events in 1150: "News arrived of the movement of the Franks upon the provinces in order to devastate and create havoc in them, and (the emirs of Damascus) set about arming to ward off their attack. The report of the plundering and enslaving carried on by the Franks in the districts of Hawran had been carried also to Nur-al-Din, who resolved upon arming to attack them, and he wrote to those in Damascus informing them of his resolve to prosecute the Holy War and demanding from them the assistance of a thousand horsemen. . . . Now they had made a treaty with the Franks to take joint action against any Muslim forces which should attack them, and therefore tried to put Nur-al-Din off with specious arguments and dissimulation. . . . He sent a message to Mujir-al-Din and the *rais* in which he said: 'It is not my purpose in occupying this encampment to seek to engage in warfare with you nor to besiege you. I have been prompted to this action solely by reason of the frequent appeals of the Muslims of Hawran and the Arab cultivators, whose possessions have been seized, whose women and children have been scattered by the hand of the Franks, and who have none to succour them. It is not possible for me, in view of the powers with which God, to him be praise, has endowed me in order to bring help to the Muslims and to engage in the Holy War against the polytheists, together with abundance of wealth and of men, neither is it lawful for me, to withhold my hand from them and from giving assistance to them, since I am aware of your inability to guard and protect your dominions, and of the remissness which has led you to call upon the Franks for assistance in fighting against me, and of your bestowal upon them of the moneys of the poor and weak amongst your subjects, whom you thus rob and defraud of their due? . . .' The answer to this letter was in these terms: 'Between us and thee there is naught but the sword, and a company of the Franks is even now on the way to aid us to repel thee, shouldst thou advance upon us and beleaguer us.' When the envoy

CHAPTER 4

returned to him with this answer and he read it, he was filled with intense astonishment and indignation at it, and determined to advance against the city. . . . But thereafter God sent heavy and continuous rains which prevented him."[12]

In light of the above, no further analysis is required. If one keeps in mind the events of a decade earlier (1140)—when the lord of Banyas, Rainier of Brus, had raided Damascene territory and robbed some flocks in violation of the treaty, King Fulk had promptly ordered the return of property and payment of compensations to the Arabs, to the satisfaction of the Damascene diplomat, Usama ibn Munqid—the success of Nur-ad-Din in the area where his father failed is rendered quite intelligible. Unlike Zangi, Nur-ad-Din was a statesman capable of organizing the political and moral integration of Arab Syria. And whereas Zangi was opposed by the effective coalition of Fulk and Unur, Nur-ad-Din had to deal with Baldwin and Mujir-ad-Din. Thus, the *modus vivendi* which had existed between Jerusalem and Damascus since 1139, and on which the future of the Kingdom of Jerusalem depended, had gradually degenerated in fifteen years, due to lack of foresight and poor leadership in Jerusalem.

Nur-ad-Din now wanted peace in order to consolidate his kingdom and to extend his institutional reforms from Aleppo to Damascus. He also thought of intervening in the wars of the Turks of Anatolia in the north, and for this reason he pacified Baldwin by continuing to pay him 8,000 dinars a year tribute money which the previous government had contracted. As for Baldwin, a year earlier, while sieging Askalon, he had given his consent to the marriage of Constance of Antioch with a turbulent young prince from the Second Crusade, Reynald of Châtillon, who was just about ready to provoke the wrath of Byzantium by outright aggression.

[12] *Ibid.*, pp. 296-99.

CRITICAL TURNING POINTS

The Revolution in the Balance of Power

The confrontation of Moslems and Christians was now reduced to two major centers of power, Aleppo and Jerusalem, with still more or less equal military potentials. The change effected by the unification of Arab Syria under Nur-ad-Din merely balanced the scales. But for the first time since the advent of the First Crusade, Moslem Syria became invulnerable through its autonomously organized resources. It had a single independent government capable of confining the Frankish power to a narrow strip along the coast line from Antioch to Gaza, with a widened bulge across the Jordan River and the Dead Sea. Adjacent to it was a similarly elongated Moslem band, stretching from north to south, but leaning against the deeper Moslem hinterland. Both sides were now in the process of increasing centralized control, while the scope of their international relations was expanding to the periphery. Thus, tendencies toward a stronger monarchy, legal reforms, and other institutional changes oriented to social integration were intensified in the two conflicting societies. These processes of internal solidarity, which reinforced the existing incompatibility of ideologies across the borderline and the sense of total threat to survival, will require a detailed sociological analysis in the next chapter. At this point attention must be focused on the enlarged scope of international relations which involved mainly Byzantium and Egypt.

If religion had been the only factor affecting international relations, and Byzantium and Egypt had been powerful empires in more than name only, then the lines would have been clearly drawn. Byzantium would interfere against Nur-ad-Din in the north, Egypt would press against Baldwin in the south, and a new balance of power would result. Neither of these peripheral powers, however, was capable of a decisive initiative in the second half of the 12th century, although both were inevitably gravitating into the Syrian system. In the course of their involvements there appeared

CHAPTER 4

elements of understanding between Byzantium and Nur-ad-Din as well as close cooperation between Egypt and the Franks, as we shall presently see. However, these cross-religious entanglements and double-cross political interests were basically symptoms of weakness on the part of the "empires." In fact, in one decade the question of Egypt became a race for its conquest between Aleppo and Jerusalem, while the Byzantines had little more than a vague premonition of their own destruction by the Fourth "Crusade" (1204). Again it must be pointed out that Nur-ad-Din had manifested greater statesmanship and resourcefulness than all the rest of the parties involved, while his rivals played into his hands in the most decisive moments. The two decades following the conquest of Damascus (1154) brought about a dramatic revolution in the balance of power in favor of Nur-ad-Din. But only his successor and those of the two kings of Jerusalem, Baldwin III and Amalric, were to reap the rewards or face the consequences. This period may be divided into two phases: first the Byzantine stalemate in the north, then the Egyptian checkmate.

Relative security in his southern frontier enabled Nur-ad-Din to take advantage of the war in Anatolia between the Saljuqid and Danishmend Turks after the death of Sultan Mas'ud (1155). He supported the Danishmends (the loosing side) and captured from Kilij Arslan II the formerly Frankish fortresses of Aintab, Duluk, and Marzban. This made him a factor in the Byzantine sphere of interest and increased his bargaining power in the coming negotiations with Emperor Manuel. Meanwhile, it provoked a temporary coalition of Kilij Arslan, Toros the Armenian, and Reynald of Antioch, which disbanded after a futile raid against Aleppo. Baldwin was somewhat occupied with Egyptian coastal raids. From June 1155 to June 1157 a signed truce was in effect between Nur-ad-Din and Baldwin. But it was broken by Baldwin early in 1157 when he raided a band of trusting Turcoman shepherds near Banyas. According to William of Tyre, the king needed money for the growing expenses of mercenary soldiers, and the booty was tremendous. This incident precipitated a series of battles. The lord of Banyas, Humphrey of Toron, could no longer defend this "profitless" frontier estate, and he handed its defense over to the Hospitallers in exchange for half of its income. En route to Banyas, a unit of the Hospitallers was ambushed and routed by the sultan's brother, Nasr-ad-Din. A bitter battle over Banyas ensued in which the main armies eventually clashed. The town was burned, but the citadel held. Then the main army of Baldwin was ambushed and defeated in Galilee and the king escaped to Safad, while a large number of lords and knights, including the Master of the Temple, were captured. In the fall of 1157 (following several severe earthquakes which damaged many fortresses, and Nur-ad-Din's illness which caused some confusion in his realm), Baldwin made an attempt to conquer Shaizar. With him were Reynald of Antioch, Raymond III of Tripoli, and Count Thierry of Flandres, who had come to the Holy Land on one of his four private crusades. But the sect of the Ismailians (Assassins) preceded them in taking advantage of vulnerable Shaizar, whose ruling family perished in the earthquake. The Franks also quarreled about whether Count Thierry, who was designated to occupy this stronghold, should pay homage to Reynald, who was of a lower rank but had a legitimate claim to the territory. When the siege was finally abandoned Nur-ad-Din promptly annexed Shaizar. The Frankish campaign was successful, however, in reconquering the important fortress of Harim for Antioch (February 1158). And later that year Baldwin made a raid on Damascus, and won a resounding victory over Nur-ad-Din at al-Butaiha upon his return from sieging the Transjordanian fortress of Habis Jaldak. During 1158 the Egyptians (whose cooperation Nur-ad-Din was seeking by repeated diplomatic contacts) raided the Jerusalem sea coast in coordination with Shirkuh's attack on Sidon. Both sides were now ready for a truce, which was made just as the armies of Byzantium, headed by Manuel, were invading Cilicia in full force. The climax of the Byzantine phase in northern Syria had been reached.

Manuel's intervention of 1158-1159 was very similar in background and structure to his father's intervention twenty years earlier. If considered as a drama in five acts, striking associations with the events of the thirties will emerge, with offspring taking the roles of ancestors.

Act One: As early as 1150 Constance of Antioch appealed to Manuel for a Byzantine candidate as her second husband, while the Franks tried to thwart this political prospect. But this time the roles were inverted. It was the Greeks who chose a middle-aged man (John Roger) whom Constance rejected (being now twenty-nine rather than a child of nine) in favor of the handsome, young (though not high ranking) Reynald de Châtillon (1153), with the approval of King Baldwin. The Byzantines were dismayed at this loss of opportunity to set a foot in Antioch. The Franks foolishly considered it a political success.

Act Two: Reynald, upon becoming regent of Antioch, dissipated his force, first against the Armenians of Cilicia (at the instigation of the Greeks), then against the patriarch Aimery whom he quarreled with and cruelly mistreated; soon after this, he installed the Templars at Alexandretta, and when the Greeks angered him for not paying him money for his Armenian campaign, he joined Toros the Armenian in an attack on the Island of Cyprus (1156). The vast plundering and devastation which resulted practically destroyed this Greek island and engendered the coming Byzantine revenge.

Intermission: (different from the events of the thirties) Baldwin made a calculated overture to Byzantium by marrying the emperor's niece, Theodora (1158), for which he received a dowry of 100,000 gold pieces. Apparently, he even made a secret agreement with Manuel that Reynald should be humiliated, but clearly had no intention of going beyond nominal concessions.

Act Three: Manuel conquered Cilicia (autumn 1158), and Reynald surrendered. At the emperor's camp, in front of many Moslem and Christian ambassadors, he was forced to perform a most humiliating ceremony: he was made to walk barefooted toward the enthroned emperor and hand over his sword, holding it by the point. "There he prostrated himself in the dust before the imperial platform, while all his men raised their hands in supplication. Many minutes passed before Manuel deigned to notice him. Then pardon was accorded to him on three conditions. Whenever it was asked of him he must hand his citadel over to an imperial garrison; he must provide a contingent for the Imperial Army; and he must admit a Greek Patriarch of Antioch instead of the Latin. Reynald swore to obey these terms. Then he was dismissed and sent back to Antioch."[13] Neither side took the "repentance" too seriously.

Act Four: Baldwin arrived with his brother Amalric at Manuel's camp for diplomatic negotiations and a possible alliance against Nur-ad-Din. On Easter 1159 Manuel made a magnificent entrance into Antioch, while some of the Franks tried to intimidate him with rumors of assassination. The procession was another fake of "friendship." "Reynald, on foot, held his bridle, and other Frankish lords walked beside the horse. Behind him rode Baldwin, uncrowned and unarmed."[14] Then followed a week of high festivities. But Manuel knew very well that the only reason the Franks were so submissive was because of the threat of Nur-ad-Din. This realization did not make him wish the destruction of Nur-ad-Din, for he knew that if he crushed the latter (assuming it was possible) the Franks would certainly not need the emperor as the protector of Antioch. Besides, Nur-ad-Din was invaluable as a proved ally against Kilij Arslan in Anatolia.

Act Five: Headed by Manuel, the combined armies of Byzantium and the Franks moved toward Aleppo in the spring of 1159. Nur-ad-Din aligned his entire forces and sent ambassadors to negotiate peace. Evidently this is what Manuel expected him to do. To the helpless disgust of the

[13] Runciman, *ibid.*, p. 352.   [14] *Ibid.*, p. 353.

CHAPTER 4

Franks, a calculated truce was soon signed. Nur-ad-Din released 6,000 Frankish prisoners, including all the captive dignitaries (among them, the Master of the Temple), and promised an offensive against the Saljuqs of Anatolia. Manuel agreed to evacuate northern Syria, and the point of a Greek protectorate over Antioch was clearly understood. The Franks were painfully disappointed and considered it another proof of Byzantine treason, but they could think of no other concrete concessions which would win Byzantium over to their specific needs. Nur-ad-Din was relieved to be left alone with Jerusalem. And Manuel had not realized that his interpretation of conventional balancing strategies was shortsighted and extremely provincial (the collapse of Fatimid Egypt was just ten years away). His real interests lay with full exploitation of the Frankish dependence upon his active engagement in northern Syria.

For a few more years things returned to their normal course. The Greeks continued their struggles against the Saljuqs of Anatolia, aided by attacks on Anatolia by Nur-ad-Din and the Danishmends, and thus regained many Greek cities and reduced Kilij Arslan to vassaldom. Nur-ad-Din captured some former dependencies of Edessa (Marash and others), while Baldwin made more raids into Damascene territory, and another truce was bought for the payment of 4,000 gold pieces. In 1160 young Joscelin of Harim and Reynald of Antioch were taken prisoners. Reynald was ambushed upon returning from a pillage raid and was imprisoned for sixteen years in Aleppo. This new emergency drew the rival forces toward Antioch, but the memory of Manuel's intervention was too fresh in Nur-ad-Din's mind. Baldwin was left free to deal with the newly complicated constitutional problems of Antioch and Nur-ad-Din went on a pilgrimage to Mecca (1161). The truce with the Moslems enabled Franks and Greeks to engage in diplomatic marriages associated with new intrigues. Bohemond III became Prince of Antioch under his mother's regency (not without Franco-Greek controversies), while his sister Maria was given in marriage to the widowed Emperor Manuel. This last event involved an offense to Raymond III of Tripoli, whose sister had been promised the hand of Manuel; Raymond avenged himself by a raid on Cyprus. All these petty developments were overshadowed by the sudden death of Baldwin in Beirut (February 1162) at the age of thirty-three. He was a great warrior but hardly a wise statesman. His main historical heritage, namely, the prevention of the unification of Syria under Nur-ad-Din, was wasted. He had gambled irresponsibly with his father's achievements in Damascus, and improved little on Fulk's failure to involve the Byzantines in northern Syria as a close ally of Jerusalem.

The career of Amalric (1162-1174) coincided with a dramatic activation of the international system involving Aleppo, Jerusalem, Cairo, and Constantinople. Egypt was rapidly drifting into chaos and impotence.[15] As a power vacuum it presented two alternative courses of action to its northern neighbors: either leave it alone by mutual agreement, thus maintaining the existing balance-of-power; or fight over it with a view to acquiring a cogent advantage in the international system. The contending parties drew each other into a showdown.

As early as 1160 Baldwin considered an invasion of Egypt, but refrained in return for a yearly tribute of 130,000 dinars (or a promise of one). In 1163 two wazirs, Shawar and Dirgham, were fighting a civil war in Egypt. Dirgham had the upper hand and Shawar fled to Damascus to ask for Nur-ad-Din's help. The latter hesitated because of the risk involved in such faraway expeditions and the necessity of crossing the intervening Christian lands. His general, Shirkuh, was enticed and argued the advantage of encircling the Franks; he also appeared to aspire to a realm of his own, independent of Nur-ad-Din.

Amalric resolved these Moslem hesitations by taking the initiative. In September 1163 he made a surprise attack on Egypt, using the grievance of the tribute as a pretext. His

[15] Details according to Runciman and others.

CHAPTER 4

army consisted mainly of the Hospitallers who were strong in the south and were closely associated with Amalric, the former lord of Jaffa and Askalon. From the outset, then, the Templars felt discriminated against and antagonistic toward the Egyptian project. A latent power struggle began to develop. Amalric had grand ambitions, on both a domestic level (as we shall see later) and on an international level. He had previously negotiated with the Byzantines, had helped them against the rebelling Armenians in Cilicia, and had supported the coming of the Greek general, Coloman, with a standing army to Cilicia and northern Syria. He was prepared even to relinquish Antioch. At the same time he explored the possibility of recruiting King Louis VII of France for another campaign in the east. Amalric was, then, a man of action, daring, and imaginative. He saw Egypt as a great opportunity to aggrandize the Kingdom of Jerusalem, and was ruthless in the pursuit of this goal, subordinating everything else to it. His first invasion of Egypt failed abruptly, however, when Dirgham flooded the Nile Valley by opening some dams. Nur-ad-Din attempted to benefit from the situation by invading Tripoli, but suffered a defeat from the combined forces of the northern principalities, the Greek Coloman, and some passing European knights.

The time for decision in Damascus had come. Shirkuh convinced Nur-ad-Din to intervene in Egypt on the side of Shawar, who offered major concessions and could be treated as a puppet. Shirkuh took with him a specially selected army (among them was the young officer, Salah-ad-Din), and, while Nur-ad-Din made a diversion attack on Banyas, Shirkuh's expedition passed safely through Frankish territory into Egypt (1164). Now Dirgham turned to Amalric for countervailing help, but Shirkuh overtook them and restored Shawar to power. From this position Shawar requested the departure of the Syrian army, but Shirkuh refused and took the fortress of Bilbais. Consequently, Shawar called upon the help of the invading Frankish army. Egyptians and Franks were now encircling and besieging the Syrian army at Bilbais. At this point Amalric received bad news from home: Nur-ad-Din, reinforced by troops from Mosul and Ortuqid princes, had attacked Antioch, defeated a Christian coalition of Franks, Greeks, and Armenians, and captured Bohemond III, Raymond III, Coloman, and others. The northern front was collapsing. Harim was taken; but rather than advancing on Antioch itself, which might have provoked a full-scale Byzantine intervention, Nur-ad-Din turned south and besieged Banyas. This latter move actually saved the hard-pressed Shirkuh. Amalric quickly made a truce by which both Franks and Syrians evacuated Egypt, and hastened to his northern frontier with Damascus. But he arrived too late to save Banyas from conquest. For a while there were some Armenian successes against Nur-ad-Din, but Amalric soon entered negotiations with Nur-ad-Din, ransomed the young Bohemond, and reinforced Tripoli with Thierry of Flandres, who happened to be there on his personal fourth crusade. The second round in Egypt was over. Amalric was determined to try again, and he needed Byzantine help.

When Amalric was in Antioch the emperor's envoy challenged his right to meddle in its affairs. Amalric decided to appease Byzantium at all costs. He sent an embassy to Constantinople to ask for a Greek princess for himself, and he induced Bohemond to install a Greek patriarch in Antioch. His political offer to Manuel was the division of Egypt between Greeks and Franks. The Jerusalemite Embassy was detained in Constantinople, however, for two years.

At the beginning of 1167 the third round over Egypt began. This time Shirkuh convinced not only Nur-ad-Din but also the caliph of Bagdad to try to liquidate the Fatimid caliphate in Cairo. When Shirkuh entered Egypt, he met the united armies of Cairo and Jerusalem. Cairo became a full-fledged protectorate of Amalric, with a tribute of 400,000 besants and a Frankish garrison in Cairo. A series of major battles ensued between the Franco-Egyptian coalition and Shirkuh, in which Alexandria was taken by Salah-

CHAPTER 4

ad-Din, and then besieged by Amalric. But no side was winning the war, and Nur-ad-Din was again active in Syria. Shawar mediated between Shirkuh and Amalric, and again both sides agreed to depart from Egypt. But this time Egypt remained allied with the Franks, and even tolerated a Frankish high commissioner in its capital. Thus Amalric had practically won this round. But his ambition was to destroy Moslem Egypt completely, and for this he needed more preparation.

During 1167 the defense of the Kingdom was reorganized, with major responsibilities assumed by the religio-military orders. In fact, most of the lands of Antioch and Tripoli were divided between the two Orders, along with many positions in Jerusalem. Amalric's bride, Maria, arrived from Constantinople, and he married her. He sent William, Archbishop of Tyre, to negotiate an alliance for a combined Franco-Greek conquest of Egypt. This time Manuel made his territorial terms clear, and a pact was signed by which operations were to start late in 1168.

But the fourth round over Egypt got out of hand. Rumors came from Egypt about the precariousness of Shawar's status and about new intrigues with Syria. Thus a Frankish emergency council was gathered in Jerusalem. The Master of the Hospital, Gilbert of Assailly, seemed to have more influence there than the king himself. While Amalric preferred to wait for the Byzantine expedition, the Hospitallers swayed a majority of the lords in favor of a "do it alone" policy. The Templars strongly opposed the violation of the alliance with Egypt and refused to participate, but Amalric yielded to the majority. Orders were given and the treacherous and hasty invasion of Egypt began in October 1168. In vain did Shawar send one ambassador after another to offer concessions which might avert the war. The Egyptians decided to fight to the death. The Franks captured Bilbais and massacred the population, both Moslem and Christian Copts. The Egyptians replied by burning Fostat, the suburb of Cairo and threatening to set Cairo itself on fire. In desperation, they called upon Nur-ad-Din. Shirkuh arrived

CRITICAL TURNING POINTS

with the largest army he had ever taken to Egypt, and forced the Franks to retreat. In January 1169 Amalric fled from Egypt, leaving it in the hands of Shirkuh.

A few weeks later Shawar was betrayed and murdered by Salah-ad-Din himself. Then the unexpected happened. Shirkuh died suddenly from over-eating and his nephew Salah-ad-Din Yusuf became master of Egypt with a puppet caliph at his mercy. His political overlord was Nur-ad-Din.

The events of the next few years did not change this basic revolution in the balance of power. There was another Frankish attempt to conquer Egypt at the end of 1169, this time with the aid of a Byzantine fleet, but it failed completely. Nur-ad-Din was preoccupied with events around Mosul and could not yet foresee the forthcoming rise of Salah-ad-Din. The Franks had sent ambassadors to the kings of Europe to incite another great crusade, but to no avail. In 1171 Amalric went to Constantinople for new negotiations with Manuel. Previously he had had to repel a first attack of Salah-ad-Din on Gaza. The terms of the new treaty with Byzantium are not known, but it probably arranged for a closer dependence of Jerusalem upon Byzantium and for new expeditions against Egypt. Meanwhile, Salah-ad-Din, under orders from Nur-ad-Din, liquidated the Fatimid caliphate and proclaimed Egypt a part of the Sunni Abassid community. Before anything decisive could develop, two major heroes of the Egyptian climax died (1174): first Nur-ad-Din, and a few months later Amalric.

International Systems and Induced Functions

Effects of a Changing International Environment

The social structure of both the crusaders and Moslems did not remain unaffected in the face of their international predicaments. The problem of coping with institutionally unanticipated situations on an international plane created new social needs and some significant modifications in political leadership. However, our concern here is not only with the relationships between international conflict and social change, but also with some causal connections between institutional resistance to change and the failures of leadership under circumstances which necessitate change. Therefore, this analysis begins and ends with a crisis of social leadership. Yet the crisis, viewed as a prolonged process, is first the key or precondition to social change, and finally it becomes the grave consequence of insufficient or inadequate change.

Some problems associated with transplantation and interlockage in a different political environment were previously analyzed in terms of institutional lag and innovative functions. The "lag" resulted from the conservative application of past culture to a new international setting, and "innovative functions" represented adaptational efforts by a social movement to overcome an unanticipated security crisis. Clearly, such developments were not the product of a cumulative cultural process or of some purely endogenous evolvement of "rationality." Rather they were induced by the changing international environment. This environment may be taken as a conflict system, the parts of which make various attempts to countervail one another's power and activities. We have distinguished this type of exogenous change from the one obtained by cultural contact and the ensuing diffusion of cultural elements from one society to another. The latter is essentially a process by which some *solutions to problems* are communicated from one system to another, while the former involves the critical *introduction of problems* through political interaction which may profoundly affect the course of social development.

Now the logic of internationally induced functions may not only link internal changes in the two or more conflicting social systems, but may also explain further the reasons for the historical turning points of the conflict, as described in Chapter Four. What follows is a preliminary characterization of the process, the phases of which will then be treated in more detail.

Since the technological base of both the crusaders and their Islamic neighbors was a static factor (for the period in question), some features of social organization, especially the ones affecting solidarity (or integration), became crucial. Aside from significant variations between the feudalism of the Franks and the patrimonialism of the Saljuqs, they resembled each other in depending largely upon religion for collective identity and morale, i.e. religion as an integrating ideology. One can safely substitute the functions of religion at the time for the functions of modern nationalism, *mutatis mutandis*, and he will not be too far from the essence of the situation. It was indeed a state of pre-national sacred solidarity, of two peoples confronting each other with a mutual non-recognition of the other's right to exist. Thus from the outset the Crusades were met by a counter-crusade, namely the Moslem Jihad. If for the Franks this was a new institution, initiated and sustained by the Roman papacy, the Saljuqid rulers of Syria had only to revive it from within the traditional resources of the caliphate. These two international institutions began to feed upon one another in an ever-growing intensity, contributing to a polar stiffening of collective ideologies. It was the spirit of Holy Wars, then, which con-

CHAPTER 5

ditioned and permeated all international relations of the system in question, and induced internal struggles for legitimate political domination.

A second induced function of the changing international system was the desperate striving of political leaders to augment the size of their domains and manpower, and to centralize power and financial resources under a strong monarchy. This was first manifested in the affiliation of small political units, which was not necessarily a voluntary process. It often involved the suppression of local particularism in the name of higher values and a wider community of interests. Second, leadership became increasingly dependent upon the capacity to organize fluid financial resources in order to recruit mercenaries to be directly and permanently employed by the central government. This seemingly quantitative tendency had a latent qualitative aspect. From here there was only one step to the monopolization of the means of warfare, taxation, and administration by a central authority. For, under the pressure of emergencies, certain traditions were bypassed or reformed by self-assertive and militarily strong leadership. As the weakness of the fragmented aristocracy was exposed, its members came under political attack from the inside and were pushed to entrenchment in the traditional institutions of legitimate order. But their positions vis-à-vis the international system grew precarious. This crisis of leadership was bound to be resolved differently under Christian feudalism than under Moslem patrimonialism, as we shall see later. However, the crisis was generated by the international system, and the adequacy of change on both sides must be measured in relation to the capacity to cope with the conditions and dynamics of that system.

Interlockage in a conflict system, especially where extreme ideological incompatibility and a total threat to existence prevail, may not only sustain a sacred polarization and political centralization, but may also induce the formation of charismatic movements oriented toward changes in social leadership. Such movements may infuse their strained societies with idealism and adaptational innovations, thus challenging the leadership of the conventional elites. In the Kingdom of Jerusalem the religio-military orders were precisely this type of movement. Similar, although not identical, were the religio-educational, legal, and welfare groups which flourished in Syria under Nur-ad-Din. If Nur-ad-Din personified the Jihad, it was not only because his armies engaged the "infidels" in battle, but mainly because of the active encouragement which he gave to these movements. Their political importance is evidenced by the fact that city after city sided with Nur-ad-Din even before their submission to him, and at times against the will of their local chieftains. However, these movements, Christian as well as Moslem, differed with respect to the degree of congruence with the established form of stratification and political domination in their respective societies.

In summary, then, the present analysis is concerned with three basic induced functions of the international system as they were reflected in the efforts of individual participants *to cope* with their international problems:

1) the mutual reinforcement of a spirit of holy wars, crusades, and jihads, which produced a pre-national, militant ideology and a collective solidarity;

2) a growing tendency to monarchical centralization, induced by the search for extra-feudal resources and by the increased need for powerful leadership;

3) the appearance of charismatic movements capable of infusing the political system with idealism and adaptational innovations, and threatening thereby the leadership positions of conventional elites.

Cultural Contact and Diffusion

"Consider and reflect on how God has in our times changed West into East. For we, who were occidentals, have now become orientals. The man who was a Roman or a Frank has, in this land, been turned into a Galilean or a Palestinian. He who was once a citizen of Reims or of Chartres has now become a citizen of Tyre or of Antioch.

CHAPTER 5

We have already forgotten the places where we were born; many of us either do not know them or have never even heard of them. One among us now has his own houses and retainers, just as if he possessed them through hereditary or family right. Another takes as his wife, not a woman of his own stock, but rather a Syrian or Armenian, or even, occasionally, a Saracen who has obtained the grace of baptism. . . . One man may possess vineyards, while another has farms. Men address one another in turn in the speech and idiom of various languages. The several languages of various nations are common here and one joins faith with men whose forefathers were strangers. . . . He who was a foreigner is now just like a native. The interloper has been made into a resident. We are followed here, from day to day, by our neighbors and parents, who abandon, though reluctantly, all their possessions. Those who were needy have here been enriched by God. Those who had a few pennies, here possess countless besants. He who had not a village, here possesses a God-given city. Why should one who has found the East to be like this return to the West? Nor does God wish to burden with poverty those who have vowed to follow him with their crosses."[1]

Fulcher of Chartres conveyed in the above words the early sense of achievement and orientalization of the Franks in the east. Other contemporary sources indicate an impressive degree of material improvement, and, in modern terms, the diffusion of cultural elements.

In architecture the Frankish aristocracy adopted the use of marble walls and painted ceilings, mosaic floors and glass windows, houses provided with baths and water brought by aqueducts, sewerage systems. Their fortresses were inspired by Arab and Byzantine models, with oriental engineers, masons, and artists contributing their skills. They started using carpets and wall hangings, carved tables and coffers, bed and table linen, porcelain dishes, and even gold and

---

[1] Fulcher of Chartres, *Historia Hierosolymitana* (tr. by James A. Brundage), Vol. III, *The Crusades, A Documentary Survey* (Marquette University Press, 1962), p. 468.

silver place settings. They availed themselves of oriental pottery, dyes, soap manufactured by urban natives, and other luxurious imported commodities.

In clothing, both men and women adopted local customs and elegant styles. At home a knight would dress in silks trimmed with fur, a long oriental tunic, and turban. Outdoors he covered his head with the Arab *kuffieh* and overcoat, his beard cut in oriental fashion. Many women were veiled like Moslem women and confined to the home, even to the extent of avoiding church services, according to the wish of jealous husbands. Local food customs were likewise adopted, including the lavish use of oriental spices, sugar, and olive oil, hardly known to the Franks before then. They relied heavily on eastern doctors and medicine, including native nurses and professional mourners at funerals. Some barons kept black slaves, dancing girls, and eunuchs, indulging at times in drunken orgies and other forms of entertainment. Even some of the patriarchs were known to maintain a Turkish harem or a mistress, one of whom was sarcastically referred to as "the Patriarchess." Many of them studied Arabic literature and learned the language. A majority of the non-noble classes intermarried with native Christians or converted Moslems, producing a hybrid group known as the *"poulains,"* whose socio-cultural characteristics were more congruent with Middle Eastern culture than with European.

Finally, agricultural production was managed almost entirely by oriental villagers, using their own techniques and supervised by their own chiefs. These subordinated village communities provided much of the material resources upon which the Frankish society depended for its livelihood.

Yet no amount of orientalization by cultural diffusion could abolish the religio-political gulf between Christians and Moslems. Their states still maintained a fundamental denial of each other's right to exist. Hence, the real base upon which the Frankish society stood was its organized knightly class, with their castles, weapons, and skills. To describe the way in which this class applied its past culture to its new setting, the problems and vicissitudes encountered through this endeavor, and the consequences of its efforts to overcome these problems, is to describe a social structure in concrete time. For the viability of any social structure is relative to its capacity to change either its external conditions or iself, or both.

Applying Past Culture to a New Situation

By the time leadership roles had passed to the second generation of crusaders (roughly coinciding with the accession of King Fulk in 1131), the following adjustments in social stratification were well-incorporated into the transplanted feudalism of the Franks.

A CITY-DWELLING CASTE OF WARRIORS

To the traditional semi-caste structure of lords and serfs a religious and ethnic cleavage was added. In no sense was the Frankish lord part of his village community, regardless of whether its population was Moslem or native Christian. In the first place, he did not possess any private land that would be tended by "his" peasants. Moreover, he dwelt in a distant fortified town, together with other lords, and had no regular social intercourse with his villagers. He simply exploited a conquered community from a distance, converting much of his dues in produce into money, and allowing the villagers a great deal of autonomy. They were governed by their own customs, led by a native chief (*rais*), and supervised by a representative of the lord (dragoman). To the native villagers this arrangement was quite consistent with past military occupations, but to the Frankish aristocracy it represented a significant change from the normal feudal mode of life. They became a city-dwelling caste of professional warriors, alienated by religion and race, and completely segregated from their conquered peasants. Though they spent much of their time in military campaigns or vigilance, they lost some typical features of a dispersed but self-sufficient country aristocracy.

"MONEY FIEFS"

While the feudal principle of "no land without a lord" was maintained, there were many lords without land, who were assigned specified revenues from ports, markets, roads, and similar facilities, in return for military service. Since these vassals were also city-dwellers, their mode of life did not differ much from that of those who held land grants. What they all had in common was the duty of unlimited military service (rather than the customary forty days a year in a circumscribed locality) under the threat of automatic loss of their fief in the event of absence for one year. There were other regulations aimed at maximizing the supply of fighting men, such as inheritance laws preventing the massive accumulation of property by a few; laws allowing a daughter to inherit a fief in default of male heirs, providing that she married an approved knight. There was also some relaxation of hereditary qualifications for knighthood, so that more of the pilgrims could be recruited and persuaded to settle in the Kingdom.

BARONIAL OLIGARCHY AND A LOW PYRAMID

Another special feature of the Jerusalemite nobility was the absence of a knightly middle stratum, such as the relatively independent English squires, for example.[2] As a result of smaller land units per knight, numerous money fiefs, and the segregation of knights from village communities, the feudal pyramid of Jerusalem was very low. It consisted of a bulk of obedient, humble knights at the bottom, serving a few great lords at the top. Thus there were, in addition to the royal domain and limited church lands, four chief fiefs and twelve lesser fiefs which covered the entire territory of the Kingdom. This kind of class differentiation resulted in two structural dispositions. On the one hand, an oligarchy of strong barons was formed side by side with the king. (Eventually it would become extremely influential in

[2] For a detailed analysis of the point see, J. Prawer, *A History of the Latin Kingdom of Jerusalem*, Vol. I (The Bialik Institute, 1963), 370-72.

CHAPTER 5

legislation and policy making, and would obstruct attempts at monarchical centralization.) On the other hand, the lower part of the knightly class became a politically weak semi-mercenary force attached to their chiefs and increasingly open to mobility from still humbler strata. It was relatively easy for a bourgeois of European descent to attain knighthood in Jerusalem and join the garrison of some lord. The Kingdom depended a great deal upon the steady recruitment of settlers from among the European pilgrims of all classes who flocked into the Holy Land twice a year. For some of these pilgrims it offered not only an opportunity for social mobility, but also a refuge from some personal trouble, such as the law.

A MILITANT CLERGY AND FIGHTING MONKS

The ecclesiastical establishment was considered part of the nobility as in feudal Europe. But in Jerusalem it was more closely involved in military functions. From the patriarch down to the archbishops, bishops, and abbots, all owed military personnel for their holdings. Together with urban communities, they provided the army with sergeants (foot soldiers) for special campaigns, and they often took command of emergency activities against surprise raids. The Church prelates participated in the Haute Cour, and, in view of the fact that policy was aimed at enemies of the Church, were more likely to give belligerent counsel.

The Church, too, became differentiated in response to the frontier situation of the Kingdom and the ever-pressing need for extra-feudal resources. The religio-military orders (whose rise and development was discussed in Chapter Three) started turning monks into knights by the hundreds, and, in the course of time, by the thousands. As pointed out earlier, they combined the divergent roles of the secular and religious nobility in an innovative way. Cultivating the spirit of unconditional service to a collective political cause, they unconsciously approached the Platonic ideal of a class of "guardians," whose status was based on achieved personal merit rather than on ascribed hereditary privilege.[3] Politically speaking, they were more disposed to a centrally regimented monarchy than any other segment of the aristocracy, including the king himself. Their military contribution became so indispensable that neither conventional vassalage nor the established Church could prevent their active participation in political leadership.

Essentially this movement embodied the most innovative way by which the Jerusalemite feudalism adapted its past culture to its new international setting.

Institutionally Unanticipated Functions

In the light of the above changes in the nature of feudal stratification, one can see that the feudalism of the crusaders was a strained one. To a degree, the imported institutions of the Franks were pre-adapted to precarious security conditions. For did not Western feudalism originate in the frontiers of an invaded civilization? Was it not, then, a form of social organization which proved effective in withstanding alien intrusions and internal disorder? But there is a difference between a defensive frontier and an offensive one, especially when the latter is advancing upon a settled population and must establish an occupation regime. Precisely that which made Frankish feudalism adequate in its European setting made it inadequate in its overseas setting. For, considered in the context of its new international system, the Jerusalemite feudalism was up against institutionally unanticipated situations. This may be further illustrated by observing two fundamental discrepancies between past and present situations.

In the first place, the institution of vassalage, in contrast to its international functions in feudal Europe, was completely useless for regulating relations with any Moslem state. We have seen that even though Jerusalem and Damascus shared a common threat—Zangid expansionism—no dependable affiliations could be established between

[3] "It is the best man, not the man of noblest birth, who is most highly prized" (St. Bernard).

them. During the crucial period of 1139-1154 Damascus was to Jerusalem an ally, a protectorate, a target for a major crusade, an object of raids for plunderings, and a neutral state. The same pattern is typical with respect to other Moslem units, such as Shaizar, the Ismailian sect, and even Egypt. Since they were all oscillating between regional accommodation and the alternative of imperial Islamic solidarity, the compulsive inconsistency of the Franks (as described in Chapter Four) was no minor factor in the ultimate choice which Moslem units had to make. As to relations with the Byzantine empire, we have also seen that vassalage was essentially unacceptable to all Latin principalities, despite vital common interests. Under pressure they would give lip-service to the emperors, but would break trust at the first opportunity. Even with Armenian principalities vassalage did not function well as an affiliating device. Obviously, it remained an introverted European institution, and thus was instrumental only in that international system. For the crusaders in the east, then, vassalage turned out to be an internally functional but externally disfunctional institution.

What was true of vassalage was even more true of religion as a social institution. If in the European setting the Church was responsible for the Peace of God and the Truce of God, in the east it was a force pressing for the War of God. In Europe it contributed to feudal coexistence, to conjunctive international relations. In the Middle East, naturally, its role was disjunctive, militant, and belligerent. At times when the secular leadership was somewhat inclined to expedient accommodations with neighbors, the religious leadership opposed this tendency with rigid intransigence. Thus in addition to the "spirit of crusades," it disinherited the Greek Orthodox Church and alienated the Syrian Christian churches. The question of the Greek patriarchate in Antioch was one of the major barriers to an alliance with Byzantium, while the question of tithes proved an unfortunate obstacle to the immigration of Armenians into Jerusalem. The Hospitallers participated in the slaughter of the

Christian Copts in Egypt, and the Templars killed the ambassadors of the Ismailian sect after they had reached an agreement for close cooperation with King Amalric (1172). More so than vassalage, then, religion contributed to the belligerent isolationism of the Franks in the East. Considered in the context of international relations the Church too was an internally functional but externally disfunctional institution.

In turning now to induced functions of the international system, it will be necessary to consider the articulation of various leadership forces with one another. Some significant differences in political orientation existed between the kings, the baronial oligarchy, the Church, and the religio-military orders. The major source of problems was the international system of the Kingdom of Jerusalem. As each one of these ruling groups differed in vantage point regarding the ways of coping with this system, so also they varied in their respective contributions to social change. Therefore, the sharing of leadership or the struggle for power between these four distinctive groups must be considered in the context of the changing international system.

Coping with International Conflict

I: THE FUNCTIONS OF HOLY WARS

Our first internationally induced function concerns the inflamed and polarized solidarity brought about by the ideology and practice of Holy Wars. From the vantage point of the Roman Church the recovery of the Holy Land was essentially an act of theocratic significance. It involved the working out of certain fundamental aspirations which had been in process for centuries. First, the old pacifistic anticipation of a second coming of Christ and the millennium was replaced by the activistic spirit of the crusades, with the "soldiers of God" now enacting a rather new drama in Jerusalem. Thus the idea of a spiritual New Jerusalem, a pure and perfect City of God, had become confused with the concrete Jerusalem as a conquered City of Man. Yet

CHAPTER 5

between the earthly ideals of feudal knighthood and the theocratically disposed Church there was no question of creating a messianic or utopian society on earth—Christian feudalism seemed good enough. Second, the spirit of the Crusades created a sharp distinction between feudal war and Holy War—*"homicidia"* and *"malicidia"*—which opened the way for those who were forbidden by canon law to shed blood to participate in "legitimate war." On the surface, this simply signified efforts at suppressing hostility within the Christian commonwealth and directing it outwards. Thus participation in a crusade carried with it salvation and great rewards for laymen's souls. But the latent effect of this new norm was to suggest the possibility of a synthesis between monastic and knightly roles, as eventually took place in Jerusalem. Third, feudalism was to be welded together and perfected by the ideal of an empire guided by the Church and destined in its crusading expansion to inherit the earth. Exactly what the status of Jerusalem was to be in this large scheme never became quite clear. It was probably closer in spirit to the Moslem concept of world domination than to the self-enclosed Judaic idea. However, as a frontier outpost of the Christian commonwealth, Jerusalem was in a position to inspire a sacred pre-national devotion in many Christians. It offered a collective ideal worthy of fighting and dying for, reinforced by the ascription of holiness to a country which had to be defended against a fierce enemy. This was indeed "feudalism-with-a-difference," or rather, feudalism approaching a purposeful synthesis with religion.

It is against this background that one can appreciate the persistent movement of enthusiastic crusades and pilgrimages. Far from being self-sufficient (let alone a profitable colony), the Kingdom of Jerusalem was in fact a supported state. Europe provided it with manpower, money, weapons, fleets, and, above all, with moral support. This infusion of sustenance would have been inconceivable without Jerusalem's special significance to Christians, namely, without the ideological influence of the Church.

Yet if the crusading movement brought the Kingdom of Jerusalem into existence and sustained it throughout, it also brought upon the Kingdom a countermovement bent on its annihilation. By the middle of the 12th century, one of the four Latin principalities in the east, Edessa, was wiped out, and the Second Crusade was called to salvage the Holy Land. But, as we have seen, in its ill-advised attack on Damascus it only encouraged more Islamic jihads, which further aided Nur-ad-Din in the unification of Syria. This mutual reinforcement of the crusading movement and the Jihad movement became a vicious circle. On the one hand, it undermined the far-sighted policy of King Fulk, who sought a *modus vivendi* with small Moslem principalities. On the other hand, were not King Fulk and his successors increasingly dependent on the permanent crusade carried on by the religio-military orders, which became the equivalent of a standing army?

In this context, it appears that the kings of Jerusalem were compelled to share leadership with the Church in a very real way. It is not a question of whether patriarchs and bishops were politically strong. Constitutionally, their position was similar to what it would have been in a regular feudal kingdom. And when two exceptional patriarchs, Daimbert and Etienne, tried to seize power, they were put down by force. Nevertheless, the Church as an institution controlled the political destiny of the Kingdom, and determined the religious framework within which the kings conducted the affairs of state. Due to the special circumstances of Jerusalem, Christian solidarity there provided more than a system of values and norms in support of legitimate government. It actually fixed and upheld Jerusalem at the center of the larger system of conflict between Islam and Christendom, while, at the same time, pushing it to the inevitable encirclement in the frontier. Thus Jerusalem's course of action could hardly break away from the effects of crusades and jihads, without repudiating the very corevalues which sustained it. In time, especially during the second half of the 12th century, the kings of Jerusalem were obliged to share leadership with the religio-military orders, including the conduct of diplomacy, international agreements, and military affairs.

This Christian collective solidarity, it must be recalled, did not integrate such available peoples as the Jacobites of Syria, the Maronites of Lebanon, the Armenians of Cilicia, the Nestorians of Iraq, the Copts of Egypt, not even the Greek Orthodoxies of the Levant. Here is perhaps one of the clearest expressions of institutional lag, or, in other words, of the failure of leadership to change a cultural pattern even under a crisis which necessitates change. The uncompromising dominance of the Roman Church and the caste values of the Frankish nobility were the institutional (or mental) barriers to the possibility of overcoming their grave deficiency in manpower.

In writing his history of the Kingdom of Jerusalem, William, Archbishop of Tyre (and a native of the Kingdom), spoke of "an insistent love of my country." He felt obliged to accept this assignment from King Amalric at a time of crisis against all personal disadvantages because "for her, if the needs of the time demand, a man of loyal instincts is bound to lay down his life." On this, the modern translators of William's work aptly remark: "Such an expression of devotion to the abstract ideal of a 'nation' is very unusual in the 12th century, when feudal loyalty to person still prevailed almost everywhere. Only the church had commanded such abstract loyalty. . . . [it was] one of the earliest and clearest instances of the expression of nationalism."[4] Moreover, one may reasonably add that in Jerusalem the conflict system of Holy Wars conditioned the mentalities of many of William's contemporaries and produced a similar devotion to country in them. William of Tyre's views might be taken, then, as *typical* of the Christian population in the Holy Land. However, on the Moslem side, too, an appropriate expression of religiously inspired pre-national solidarity was evoked and intensified by the conflict system.

[4] William of Tyre, *A History of Deeds Done Beyond the Sea* (tr. by Babcock and Krey) (Columbia University Press, 1943), p. 55.

INTERNATIONAL SYSTEMS & INDUCED FUNCTIONS

II. THE FUNCTIONS OF CENTRALIZATION

The second effect of the international system concerns the crisis of traditional leadership and the significant, although not decisive, development of monarchical centralization.

Professor John La Monte concludes his systematic study of feudal monarchy in Jerusalem with the following paradoxical observations:[5] "... in no country of western Europe is such *pure feudalism* to be found for so extended a period of time as it is in the crusading states. In the West the encroachments of the royal power and the development of absolutisms modified and eventually destroyed the feudal states. In the East the feudal decentralization lasted throughout the life of the kingdom, and was largely responsible for its final destruction. . . . I do not think that the monarchs of Jerusalem were unaware of their position; the attempts of Amaury to modify feudalism prove that the kings would have liked to establish that centralization of government which was so needed in their country; but the feudal principles of government were too strongly embedded. . . . It has been shown that the decentralization of the feudal organization weakened and in part precipitated the fall of the crusading states. Yet when one considers that they lasted for almost two centuries it must be admitted that there were in feudalism elements of strength; . . . Perhaps the barons of Outremer were wise; feudalism had been generated as a system for securing protection and some sort of government in adverse circumstances. Under feudalism the crusading states managed to keep alive. Can one say that the experiment failed altogether and that pure feudalism may not have been, in the circumstances, the most practical and permanent form of government?"

This paradoxical note of empathy cannot undo La Monte's own penetrating analysis of the fatal resistance to change by the feudal caste in Jerusalem. However, the ques-

[5] John L. La Monte, *Feudal Monarchy in the Latin Kingdom of Jerusalem* (Cambridge University Press, 1932), p. 243.

tion is not only whether the crusading states fell *because of* their feudalism or *in spite of* their feudal consistency. It seems more useful to ask in what context was their special feudalism prevented from developing along lines similar to European principalities, and what determined their peculiar (not just "pure") developments.

From the vantage point of the kings and barons of Jerusalem, the greatest problem presented by the international system in which they were interlocked was the abnormality of a small territory requiring a disproportionately large army for its defense. Here was not only "feudalism with a difference," but a basic crisis. For if it was easy to impose, in a conquered country, the norm of "no land without a lord," it was not as simple to organize and sustain a sufficient amount of lords-without-land in order to meet the challenges of numerically superior enemies. Indeed, as an outpost of Christianity against Islam, Jerusalem acquired an unconventional supply of manpower, but its only institutionally known way of incorporating fighting manpower was the feudal benefice system. This meant two things: first, a compulsive dependence upon territorial expansion; and second, a maximal utilization of extra-agricultural resources in the form of money fiefs. Both of these measures characterized the partly successful policy of the early kings. But when this expansion was contained and some territories were lost to the unifying forces of Syria under Nur-ad-Din, the problem of manpower grew beyond the reach of feudal organization. At this point the situation required a definite increase in military capacity, while conventional resources for attaining it were diminishing. This was the crisis of traditional leadership.

Under such international circumstances there could not be a greater stimulus or opening for some form of extra-feudal military organization. Consequently the king, as a leading statesman, received the eager consent of the feudal High Court to recruit as many mercenary soldiers as he could finance, and regardless of the consequences to the internal feudal balance of power. Undoubtedly that was the reason why the religio-military orders were not prevented from occupying such prominent military positions in the Kingdom as they did. There was, then, a situation much conducive to monarchical centralization, but not quite comparable to that of the later Capetian kings in France. There the kings, as powerful feudal *seignors*, were selfishly motivated to extend their domain at the expense of autonomous principalities and baronies. Therefore, it was necessary for them to achieve a superior command of extra-feudal financial and military power, thus gradually enforcing a supra-feudal authority and administration. In Jerusalem, however, the internal struggle for power was definitely conditioned by the international conflict system. In contrast to the regional particularism characteristic of many European barons, or the "cosmopolitan individualism" of some errant knights, the Jerusalemite barons and their men lived in a besieged country facing extermination in default of unity. Accordingly, they were induced to interpret feudal customs in the direction of strict corporate discipline and swift collective action. But this does not mean that feudal structure was breaking down, or that the kings entertained absolute personal leadership. For if feudal *cooperation* was at a maximum, it is not surprising that so were the values of feudal *autonomy*. Personal autonomy may lose its social support only when it appears detrimental to social solidarity, not when it contributes to it. Thus, paradoxical as it may sound, there developed in Jerusalem some de facto centralization of power which operated through feudal mechanisms of political integration. The famous *assise sur la ligece* of King Amalric shows in what direction the need for monarchical centralization was most likely to be expressed.

In 1163, a simple knight was arbitrarily dispossessed of his fief by Gerard, the Lord of Sidon. The matter was appealed to King Amalric, who promptly reinstated the knight with the approval of the High Court. He then pressed the High Court, which was composed of direct vassals of the king, into passing an assise which linked all the sub-vassals

CHAPTER 5

personally with the king by liege homage. This law represented a significant victory of the king and the simple knights over the grand barons. For in one stroke it made all fief-holders in the Kingdom peers of each other, both in relation to the king and in relation to the High Court. The tenants-in-chief still retained their status of intermediary links between the king and all those who did not hold benefices directly from him, but their control of their own vassals ceased to be exclusive. Legally speaking, it converted the knightly class as a whole into a corporation presided over by the king, with the barons as sort of district commanders. If a *seignor* had a conflict with one of his vassals, he was obliged to demand justice from the body of all his vassals, while this body of equals could bring any grievance against their lord to the king (as a common seignor) and his High Court. Thus the assise protected the *arrière* vassals against their *seignors* while also supporting the king against dissenting barons by committing their men directly to the king. But the latent function of this law contained the seeds of constitutional monarchy, for it could be applied against arbitrary rule by the king himself and limit his authority to the consent of the High Court.

This unprecedented reform in feudal structure was probably not so much a result of Amalric's "absolutist" tendencies (it took place in the first year of his accession to the crown) as it was a reflection of the gradual exposure of the weakness of the baronial aristocracy vis-à-vis the international situation of the Kingdom. Their fragmented authority declined as the military crisis of the Kingdom mounted. As we have seen, King Fulk and Baldwin III had begun to assert greater leadership by supplementing the feudal host with standing mercenary forces and the religio-military orders. They had unconventional financial means at their disposal, such as tributes from Moslem protectorates, donations, special levies, and they often resorted to plundering campaigns. On the other hand, the functional importance of every single knight did not decrease, and their fighting morale was vital. Thus the alliance of the king with the body of simple knights became both possible and necessary. Amalric inherited from his brother a unified Syria and the danger of further encirclement by the forces of Nur-ad-Din moving into Egypt. His time demanded a monarchy equal in military capacity to the rising Moslem monarchy, but despite his ambitions in this direction he figured more as a military adventurer than a reforming statesman. His revolutionary assise, which could have marked the very early beginning of a centralized monarchy, served later as a legal pretext for baronial usurpation of power. A lack of dynastic continuity combined with extremely low-ranking knights, would leave the High Court to powerful barons acting as peers against any class-transcending authority. Immediately after Amalric's death, his seneschal and major advisor, Miles de Plancy, who intended to continue the policy of centralization, was murdered. The barons were openly accused in this political assassination.[6]

After describing some personal faults of Amalric, such as seduction of married women, greedy encroachments upon churches, appropriation of "gifts" from various sources, William of Tyre quotes the king's excuse for his conduct as follows: "Every prince, and above all a king, should ever see to it that he is never in straitened circumstances, and that for two reasons: first, because the wealth of the subject is always safe when the ruler is not in need; secondly, that he may have resources at his disposal from which to provide for the necessities of his realm whenever an unexpected emergency arises. In such a case, the provident king should be most munificent and should spare no expense. Thus it will be plain that whatever he has he possesses not for his own benefit but for the good of the realm." On this the chronicler comments: "Even those who disliked the king could not deny that these reasons were applicable in his case. For when the kingdom was in critical straits he spared no expense.... But the wealth of his subjects was far from safe, for again and again he took advantage of the

[6] Jean Richard, *Le Royaume Latin de Jérusalem* (Presses Universitaires de France, 1953), p. 79.

CHAPTER 5

most trivial pretexts to make serious inroads upon their patrimony."[7]

That Amalric was hard pressed for money to finance mercenary forces is epitomized by the following conversation with Thoros, Prince of Armenia. The latter observed that most lands and castles of the Kingdom were owned by the religio-military orders, and inquired how the king managed to have an army at his personal service. Amalric replied that he hired troops. Then Thoros asked where he got the money, and Amalric said: "I borrow it as much as I can, my brother." And Thoros expressed his sympathy for this precarious situation.[8]

In this light it must be observed that the extension of monarchical power in Jerusalem was basically quantitative. It moved into the internal power vacuum created by the inability of the feudal aristocracy to discharge its social functions, as imposed by a changing international system. But, however close this change came to a qualitative transformation of the institutional order, the necessary preconditions for monarchical centralization were not fully developed. These may be briefly summarized as follows: (1) the idea of a nation supported by a class-transcending political organization, (2) a decisive decline of the monopoly over the means of violence by the feudal class, and a distinction between the territory of the state and the properties of this class, (3) an elaborate administration in the hands of political leadership capable of taxing a unified population, hiring governmental personnel, and utilizing an effective communication system.

As we have seen, some elements of these necessary preconditions were in the process of emergence in the Kingdom of Jerusalem. They were more conspicuously present in the religio-military orders to which we now turn.

III. THE FUNCTIONS OF SOCIAL CHANGE

The most far-reaching social change in the Kingdom of Jerusalem was accomplished by the religio-military orders.

---
[7] William of Tyre, *ibid.*, p. 298.
[8] Ernoul, as quoted by La Monte, *ibid.*, p. 163.

Earlier in this study the development of this movement was explained in terms of *institutional lag* and *innovative functions* resulting from the transplantation of feudalism into a new international system. The purpose of the following analysis is to elaborate on the connection between *international systems* and changes in social organization.

When Philip IV, King of France, destroyed the Order of the Temple in 1307, he knew what he was doing. The Orders survived the Kingdom of Jerusalem and became a "portable holy land" still sworn to the Pope. They were semi-sovereign political organizations whose *raison d'être* had disappeared, unless there was a way to integrate them with the monarchy. Moreover, they enjoyed the authority of the Church combined with something the Church never had, namely, the military power to back spiritual authority. The Templars were especially strong in France, serving as agents, treasurers, and bankers of the kings, possessing vast properties, and operating a highly advanced centralized organization. Philip showed his respect and appreciation for the Orders by first making a bid for direct personal control of them. *He demanded that the kings of France (beginning with himself) should become hereditary Grand Masters of the combined Orders.* This naturally conflicted with the interests of the papacy, even though Philip was prepared for crusading expansions in and beyond Christendom. But there could be only one central authority; it was either he or the Church. Thus, when his grandiose plan was rejected, Philip turned against the papacy and the Templars with all his might. Popes were brutalized, humiliated, and intimidated into submissive cooperation with the king; the Templars were arrested, tried for heresy, and executed by the thousands; before that, the Jews were expelled and their possessions appropriated; the nobility was subdued with the aid of bourgeois administrators and vice versa—all this with an eye to a powerful monarchy.

To what extent was Philip's original idea of integrating the religio-military orders with the monarchy feasible in the Kingdom of Jerusalem a century and a half earlier?

CHAPTER 5

In answering this question one must first take into account that military monks were a Jerusalemite phenomenon, that they emerged in response to Jerusalem's special international situation, and that they represented there an adequate alternative to a collapsing feudalism. It was the crisis of feudal leadership in the face of the gradual unification of Islam which carried this movement to positions of supreme significance. Hence there was no choice for the kings of Jerusalem between ruling or destroying this movement. If the de facto cooperation between the kings and the Orders had been carried to its logical conclusion, there probably would have come a moment of synthesis between them. In that case the entire institutional order of the Kingdom would have been reshaped in the direction pointed by the highly integrated social organization which the Orders achieved within their own ranks. Let us view first the nature of their internal structure.

The initiation ceremony of a new member included oaths to abide by the sixty-six chapters which made up the "Rule of the poor knighthood of the Temple." He thus solemnly committed himself to full *renunciation of private property*, contributing his present possessions and future gifts to the Order. He swore to a life of *celibacy* and avoidance of all contacts with women, including the kissing of relatives. He was to give up *privacy* in eating and sleeping (always two by two), in personal belongings (unlocked chests), or even in personal letters. He swore to extreme *asceticism* in daily life: two meals a day, meat only thrice a week; no engagement in sports or similar delights; no bathing for long periods; sleeping with clothes on, and never without light during the entire night ("lest the dark enemy is thus given some opportunity"); getting up at midnight to hear Matins and say numerous paternosters; getting up at sunrise for more prayer and work; waiting until noon for breakfast; always inhibiting idle conversation ("Life and death are in the hands of the tongue"). And, above all, strict obedience to the Master or his commanders was required, with severe punishments for disobedience.

"You must entirely renounce your own will—
And entirely submit to that of another—
You must fast when you are hungry—
Keep watch when you are weary—
Thirst when you would drink—

"And he who presides over the chapter shall say, 'Dear brother, you ask a great thing, for you see only the outward trappings of the order. . . . But . . . you will find it very difficult . . . to be unable to follow your own will in any thing. When you wish to be in this country, you will be sent overseas, or if you wish to be in Jerusalem, you will be sent to Tripoli, or Antioch, or Armenia. . . . Do you swear to God and Our Lady that you will all your days obey the master of the Temple and all others placed in authority over you?' And the candidate shall say, 'Yes, sir, if God pleases.'

"Then in the name of God . . . we accept you . . . as sharing the good works which have been done by the order since its foundation. . . . And we promise you bread and water, the poor mantle of the order and much hardship and labor."[9]

As the ceremony came to its close the knight would get a uniform (the white mantle with a red cross) while a priest would sing at the altar, "Behold how good and pleasant it is for brethren to dwell together in unity." And all brothers present would kiss the novice on his mouth.

With this act he was converted from a "vassal" to a "brother," i.e. from being a man-of-another-man in a contractual exchange of benefice for service, to being a member of an organization which claimed unconditional devotion to an impersonal purpose. It was a fundamental transformation. Kinship and feudal relationships were governed by ideas of what individuals *are* or *do* to *one another*. The brotherhood of the Temple was based on the will of individuals to become *instruments* of a power superior to

[9] Edith Simon, *The Piebald Standard* (Little, Brown & Co., 1959), pp. 109-10.

them. Naturally, individual motives might have been at variance with the norms and goals of the organization. Also, personal rewards were involved in the form of higher social status or in the achievement of the "crown of martyrdom." But by placing loyalty to a sacred social ideal above loyalty to any person, the basis of action had been shifted from self-seeking cooperation to self-sacrificing efforts. Nothing could better represent the latent capacity of social groups *under crisis* to transform individuals into means for the realization of self-transcending ends. And no other feudal kingdom at the time could be an object of such devotion, or have as much need for such a social organization, as the Holy Land did.

That this type of social organization saved the feudal Kingdom of Jerusalem from an early collapse due to manpower deficiency, is best indicated by the fact that when the services expected of frontier fiefs exceeded the value of such fiefs as property, secular lords were no longer capable of or interested in holding them. The Orders, however, could operate at a loss in one place by supporting it from the collectivized revenues of other places. They considered it their great mission to fill the gaps created by the retreating "private enterprise" of secular lords.[10] Hence the correlation between mounting Islamic encroachments and the growing acquisition of lands and fortresses by the religio-military orders. "In Latin Syria the exploitation of property was a precarious business," says a historian of crusading warfare. ". . . jurists considered the circumstances in which the poverty of lord or vassal temporarily destroyed the normal feudal relationship. . . . Feudal rulers could no longer discharge their responsibilities. . . . The principal beneficiaries of the situation were the military Orders; feudal poverty created a market in land of which the knights took increasing advantage."[11] Typical cases in point are: the placement

[10] See the previous discussion of this point in Chapter Three, pp. 65-70.

[11] R. C. Smail, *Crusading Warfare* (Cambridge University Press, 1956), pp. 100-01.

of Hospitallers and Templars in the frontier fortresses of Beit Jibrin and Gaza against Egyptian intrusions (1137, 1149); the settlement of Hospitallers and Templars along the dangerous boundaries of Tripoli in its major fortresses of Krak-des-Chevaliers, Safita, and Tortosa, with the right to conduct wars on their own initiative, and the commitment of Raymond II not to sign treaties with the Moslems without the Orders' consent (1142-1152); the granting of half of Banyas (the site of frequent battles and plunderings on the frontier with Damascus which the two Orders had made an unsuccessful attempt to reach in 1157 at a loss of hundreds of knights) to the Hospitallers by its weary lord, Humphrey of Toron; the installment of the Templars and later the Hospitallers in the military frontier of Antioch (which had been reduced to the Orontes River), and the ceding of such strongholds as Bagras and Marqab to them (1167, 1186).[12]

All this despite the fact that the Orders served the kings of Jerusalem as practically extra-feudal forces; they were neither formal vassals nor paid mercenaries of the kings. Beginning with King Fulk, all major campaigns of the Kingdom, whether against Moslems or internal rebellions, leaned heavily on the massive participation of the Orders. Their military significance is aptly stated by La Monte. "They were throughout most of the period of the Frankish control the most important single source of strength in the military establishment of the Kingdom of Jerusalem, and their castles and garrisons were always to be found on the borders and in the most dangerous and strategic positions throughout the Kingdom."[13]

Since the Kingdom managed to survive mainly because of the sacrifices of the religio-military orders, they gradually came to view themselves as the real leaders, if not owners, of the country which their heroic organization protected.

---

[12] For more details on this subject see Claude Cahen, *La Syrie Du Nord à l'Epoque des Croisades* (Librairie Orientaliste Paul Geuthner, 1940), pp. 510-21.

[13] John L. La Monte, *ibid.*, p. 218.

CHAPTER 5

They became a special status group, claiming a charismatic authority and challenging the customary prerogatives of the church and secular government.[14] However, the Templars and Hospitallers acted as two separate "imperialisms,"[15] jealous of each other and struggling for exclusive aggrandizement. Nevertheless, the basis for their common opposition and contempt for the traditional establishment lay in the actual social changes which they accomplished. These may be now summarized as follows:

1) A powerful segment of the knightly class became organized on a non-feudal basis, both in internal personal relationships and in relation to other bodies of the feudal hierarchy. It was a voluntary ascetic and collectivistic organization with a special purpose.

2) Since it was the only military organization with religious authority of its own and the only religious organization that was self-sufficient in military power, it actually broke the monopoly of the secular nobility over the means of warfare, and similarly the control of religious life by the ecclesiastical establishment.

3) Formally sworn only to the Roman Pope, and thus granted the privilege of sovereignty with respect to Patriarchs and kings, they enjoyed almost complete extra-territoriality. In fact, however, it was not the Pope, but the Holy Land which they served as guardians. They were, in effect, a class-transcending "liberation movement" of that land, and they protected a collectively claimed territory, not feudally bound estates.

---

[14] William of Tyre (*ibid.*, p. 239), representing the point of view of the official Church, describes at length the aggressive attitude of the Orders towards the Church and the lay authorities. Among the abuses: ringing loud bells to disturb sermons of the patriarch, shooting at the Holy Sepulchre, invading churches, giving sacraments to excommunicated persons and associating them with the Orders. The latter abuse suggests the desperate interest of the Orders in recruiting manpower. This also explains their refusal to pay tithes to the Church and their aggressive claim of booty in battles—witness the Templars in Askalon and the Hospitallers in Egypt.

[15] To use an expression of Claude Cahen's (*ibid.*, p. 521).

4) Their positions in the Kingdom of Jerusalem were not limited to any particular region and not comparable to that of regular baronies. They could concentrate manpower, and were invited to do so everywhere throughout the Kingdom, as much as their international resources enabled them. This made them a highly centralized corporation, administering large scale economic and military affairs with political priorities in mind. It thus converted them into a de facto state-within-a-state, with its own institutional order.

It is not difficult to see that all of the above developments fit very well the necessary preconditions for monarchical centralization as summarized earlier. Obviously, these were social changes induced and reinforced by the security crisis of the feudal Kingdom of Jerusalem. Thus the change from self-seeking feudo-vassalic structure to self-sacrificing instrumental brotherhood; the charismatic synthesis of the monastic and knightly roles, introducing religious significance to military action; the transformation of traditional functions of the Church and contractual ties with feudal lords, replacing them with class-transcending dedication to the venerated country; and finally, the establishment of a centralized organization capable of subordinating particular economic interests to impersonal political aspirations—all of these changes clearly had their basis in the international conflict system of the crusaders' society. That is logically corroborated by the uniqueness of such developments in comparison with contemporary feudal kingdoms. On the other hand, the parallel process of political integration achieved by the Islamic opponents points to the countervailing import of the social changes accomplished by the religio-military orders in Jerusalem. Thus the events which determined the major historical turning points (as described in Chapter Four) did reflect, to a significant degree, the relative capacity of the conflicting societies to respond with structural changes to one another, and to affect one another's social organization through needs implicated in the inter-societal system.

CHAPTER 5

There was, however, one crucial difference between the Kingdom of Jerusalem and its Islamic rivals with respect to the relationship between religion and the state. Without delving into the intricacies of this subject (the aspects of which are well known), suffice it to say that whereas Moslems were disposed to view the head of state as a natural leader of the religious community, it was not so with European Christians. The political significance of this cultural difference in regard to the empire of Salah-ad-Din will be discussed in the following chapter. In the feudal Kingdom of Jerusalem the formation of a centralized monarchy, *with the aid of the religio-military orders*, would have amounted to a theocratic revolution.[16] Nowhere in feudal Europe was the balance of power between the secular nobility and *organized religion as favorable for this revolution as it was in* the Kingdom of Jerusalem. But the almost permanent war with Islam took a heavy toll from both the Orders and the secular knights. The Kingdom depended upon the preservation of every possible source of manpower, and there was hardly a respite for any political reform. However, during the forty years which passed between the second crusade and the fall of Jerusalem it was mainly the fighting monks who supplied military reinforcements. Had King Amalric possessed the vision to use the same centralizing approach with respect to the Orders as he had in reorganizing his feudal host, he would probably have commanded a force equal to the task of containing Nur-ad-Din. Thus, for example, in 1168 the Hospitallers could not have forced him to attack Egypt before the Byzantine army had arrived, and neither could the Templars decide to back out of the campaign. As it was, the last known intention of Amalric regarding the Templars was to break this powerful and independent or-

[16] Jean Richard (*ibid.*, p. 106) mentions speculations about an attempt by the Patriarch Etienne de Chartre to establish a theocracy with the Templars as its militia, but there is no evidence for this, except that the patriarch was known for his political ambitions, which cost him his life.

ganization.[17] Had he remembered that in 1162 the Templars were strong enough to interfere in the conflict between two rival Popes (Octavian and Alexander III), and to dictate to their chosen Pope the famous Bull ("*Omne Datum Optimum*") which declared their immunity from all lay and ecclesiastical authorities, making them an autonomous church, he would have preferred to join them rather than beat them.

Thus, after the death of Amalric the Kingdom of Jerusalem was due for internal feudal rivalries, greater autonomy of the Orders in relation to the king, antagonism between the Church and the religio-military orders, and sharper competition between the Hospitallers and Templars themselves.

[17] William of Tyre, *ibid.*, p. 394.

The Collapse of the Kingdom

Manpower Deficiency and Social Structure

"We seek a man, not money. Wellnigh every Christian region sendeth us money, but no land sendeth to us a prince. Therefore, we ask a prince that needeth money, not money that needeth a prince."[1] These words of the Patriarch of Jerusalem to King Henry II of England in April 1185 reflect one of the chronic predicaments of the Latin Kingdom of Jerusalem throughout its entire history. By a "prince," of course, the Patriarch meant an army, namely, manpower. The collapse and surrender of most fortresses after the battle of Hittin two years later was clearly a result of a grave manpower deficiency. Fortified and well-populated cities do not fall overnight just because a large army has been annihilated in the field, unless there is no one left in the city to defend it. A city like Jerusalem, for example, could certainly have shown effective resistance if it had been supported by a strong militia. Only after escaping from Hittin to Jerusalem in a desperate moment did a leading baron, Balian of Ibelin, hurriedly confer knighthood on sixty "ineligible" men of the bourgeoisie so that they might help defend the city. Nothing could dramatize more strongly the connection between manpower deficiency and the existing social structure than Balian's "deviant" act. Let us turn now to an examination of the events which led to this collapse of the Kingdom of Jerusalem.

[1] Quoted by G. A. Campbell, *The Knights Templars* (Duckworth, 1937), p. 100.

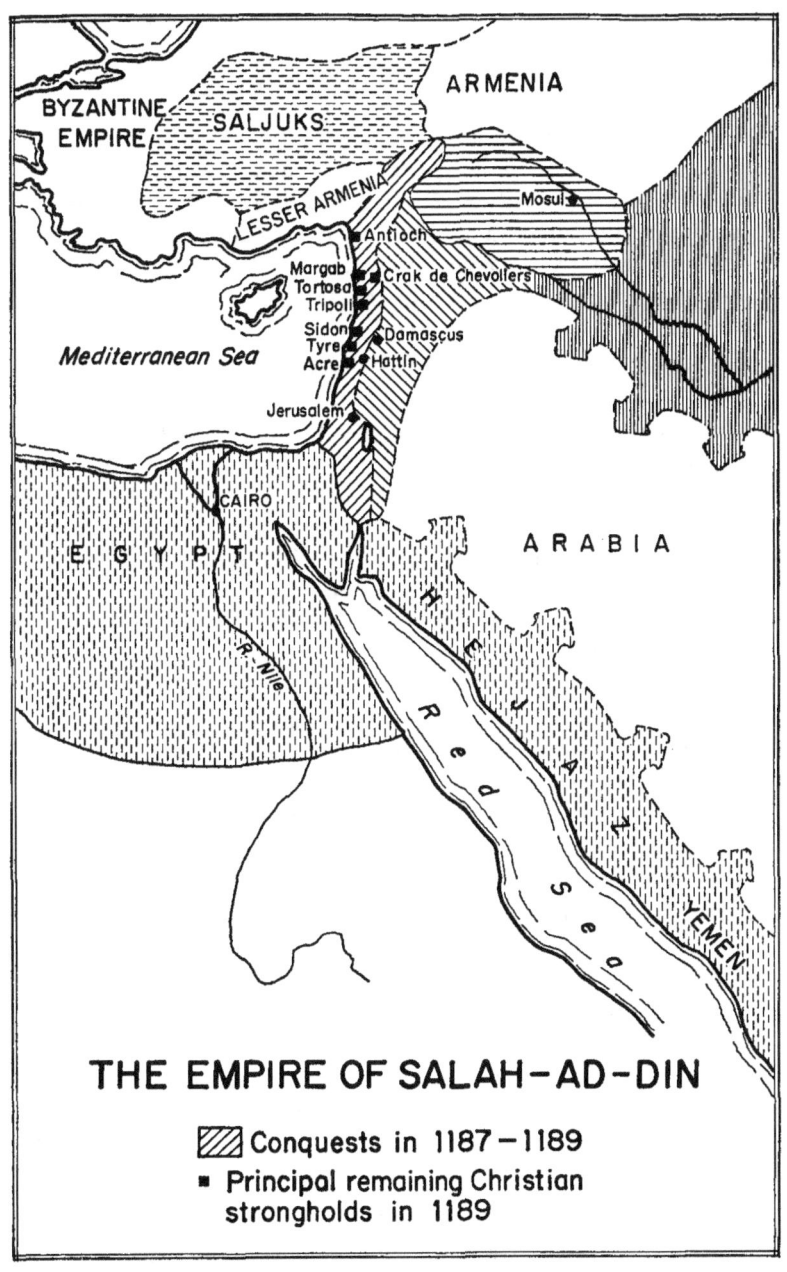

Map III: The Empire of Salah-ad-Din
Adapted from Edith Simon, *The Piebald Standard*
(Little, Brown, 1959).

CHAPTER 6

Islamic Solidarity under Salah-ad-Din

The revolution in the balance of power, which began with the conquest of Egypt by a Syrian army in 1169, was carried one step further with the liquidation of the Fatimid caliphate by Salah-ad-Din in 1171. It opened the way for Islamic unity from Cairo to Bagdad. Salah-ad-Din took this decisive action somewhat reluctantly, under orders from his suzerain Nur-ad-Din; his first concern was with consolidating his own power in Egypt. But he was thereby inadvertently placed in a most strategic position for leadership over the entire Jihad movement. Egypt was a source of tremendous revenues and manpower which, if mobilized for the cause of Jihad, would enable the Saljuqid forces of Syria to embark upon large-scale offensives against the Franks from all directions. In fact, it was larger and richer than all other provinces of Nur-ad-Din combined. Now that this "province" was drawn into the political system organized for Jihad, it was certain that its new ruler would become conscious of the key role he could play in that system. Thus, on the basis of ability to determine success or failure of the Holy War, he could eventually claim leadership over the realm of Nur-ad-Din or of Islam at large. When Nur-ad-Din and his successors realized this, it was too late to reverse the trend. Was it not Nur-ad-Din himself who had achieved the predominance of the cause of Holy War over local particularism in Syria?

That Salah-ad-Din grasped the political advantages of Jihad quite early and with a view to independence is revealed in the diploma of his investiture by the Fatimid caliph (!) as "the victorious king" and champion of Jihad as early as March 1169. This document, actually composed by Salah-ad-Din's advisor and secretary, the Qadi al-Fadil, contained the following: "As for the holy war, thou art the nursling of its milk and the child of its bosom. Gird up therefore the shanks of spears to meet it and plunge on its service into a sea of sword-points... until God give the victory which the Commander of the Faithful hopeth to be

THE COLLAPSE OF THE KINGDOM

laid up for thy days and to be the witness for thee when thou shalt stand in his presence."[2] It was not long before some independent military moves of Salah-ad-Din made Nur-ad-Din suspicious. For example, when he successfully besieged Montreal (1171) to the point of a Frankish readiness to surrender, and Nur-ad-Din came to join him, he halted the siege and returned to Egypt claiming some urgent business there. The same thing was repeated in 1173 with the siege of Kerak. Even Salah-ad-Din's own father rebuked him for these transparent tactics. But before it could come to an open rift Nur-ad-Din died in 1174, leaving a son too young to rule, and Salah-ad-Din entered the Syrian arena of succession. The Franks too had just lost their king, Amalric, and were left with a child heir and a problem of reorganization. This was Salah-ad-Din's great opportunity.

The events of the next decade or so reflect the following pattern of development:

1) Nur-ad-Din's domain breaks to pieces in the usual Saljuqid manner of succession rivalries;

2) Salah-ad-Din, as a champion of Jihad, concentrates mainly on disinheriting the broken Zangid dynasty in Damascus, Aleppo, and Mosul, while building a larger empire;

3) The Kingdom of Jerusalem plunges into a series of internal conflicts, while failing to exploit effectively the desperate invitations of Zangid rulers to cooperate against Salah-ad-Din;

4) The Byzantine empire suffers a major defeat from the Saljuqs of Asia Minor and is thus eliminated from the relevant international system, while no serious European reinforcements arrive in the Holy Land;

5) Finally, Salah-ad-Din emerges as the leader of a vast integrated military structure facing an isolated and demoralized feudal kingdom.

[2] Quoted by H.A.R. Gibb, "The Rise of Saladin," in Setton and Baldwin (eds.), *A History of the Crusades*, Vol. II (University of Pennsylvania, 1958), p. 564.

CHAPTER 6

Perhaps the factor which accounted most for this development was the religious and moral rearmament of the Syrian urban population (in reaction to the Christian crusades) which had originally been cultivated by Nur-ad-Din, and found its champion in Salah-ad-Din. The rural population of either side could not figure very much in the international conflict. It could not resist anywhere the power of the mounted military units of either the Saljuqs or the Franks. Neither could these alien ruling groups draw their manpower from a free peasantry with a national *esprit de corps*. Hence the system of political domination was based upon exploitation of the countryside from a network of castles, while drawing legitimacy from the ideology of the dense urban population, whose massive support was necessary for defending huge walls and for financing extensive military activities.[3] In these centers of power the moral support of the Fukaha (jurists-theologians), the Sufi Orders (monastic fraternities), the leaders of Madrasas (religious colleges), and other educational and welfare institutions was vital for any effective government. In closely aligning political leadership with religious aims, Nur-ad-Din and his not-hereditary successor, Salah-ad-Din, succeeded in overthrowing dissenting local emirs, and having the gates of strongly fortified cities opened before them by the force of public opinion. Thus they were able to use even the *waqf* funds (money designated for charitable religious aims) for military fortifications and general financing of Jihad. On the other hand, they abolished all taxes which were not sanctioned by Islamic law. It is this prenational religious solidarity of the urban population which explains why Salah-ad-Din did not have to really conquer Syrian cities but only perform a show of force in their vicinity, while fighting very few decisive battles against the

---

[3] Ibn Jubair, the famous Moslem traveller, who passed between Damascus and Acre in 1184, noticed that the Moslem villagers fared better under the Franks than under Moslem rulers in the area (*Recueil des Historiens des Croisades* [Académie des Inscriptions et Belles Lettres, 1841-1906], Or. III, pp. 445-56).

THE COLLAPSE OF THE KINGDOM

standing armies (*asqar*) of rival rulers who lacked popularity with the Jihad movement. At this stage there was hardly a chance for the Franks to prevent Islamic integration and military centralization with regional balance-of-power politics, unless they could force Salah-ad-Din into an early showdown and win it decisively. But here is precisely where the relative Frankish weakness lay. They lacked a massive and loyal urban population that could be relied upon for the defense of fortified cities while, at the same time, supplying them with sufficient funds for large-scale, mobile campaigns.[4] For the Franks a major military engagement in the field involved total mobilization (the *arrière* ban) and the precarious abandonment of almost all fortified places, including the cities. Therefore, such total efforts were only undertaken for counteroffensives against dangerous invasions, and could not be directed too deeply and for too long into enemy territory. Salah-ad-Din understood his strategic advantages very well when he commented on Frankish raids into the Moslem frontier during his annexation campaigns in Mesopotamia: "While they knock down villages, we are taking cities; when we come back we shall have all the more strength to fight them."[5] His plan was very simple: as long as the Franks confined themselves to defense, he would postpone the major showdown until after the unification of Egypt, Syria, and Mosul, if not the entire Moslem commonwealth. And he was not

[4] J. Prawer, *A History of the Latin Kingdom of Jerusalem* (The Bialik Institution, 1963), pp. 460-61, estimates the entire Frankish population in the Holy Land at about 100,000-120,000. The three major cities—Jerusalem, Acre, and Tyre—were inhabited by 20,000, 40,000 and 30,000 respectively, with a high proportion of non-Franks. Other "cities" did not exceed 2,000, while many strategically located fortresses depended entirely on professional garrisons. There were about 1,200 agricultural villages amounting to 250,000 people, the overwhelming majority of whom were Moslems. On the whole, the Franks comprised about 25 per cent of the total population. They had no problem in controlling the rural areas, for reasons stated above, but their manpower resources in the cities were extremely meager.

[5] Ibn-al-Athir, quoted by R. C. Smail, *Crusading Warfare* (Cambridge University Press, 1956), p. 37.

CHAPTER 6

going to achieve unification with sheer brutality or treacherous tactics (as Zangi). His model was Nur-ad-Din, and he sought legal recognition of his mission from the caliph at Bagdad, moral support from all religious leaders, and personal appreciation from officers and soldiers.

The first issue in Syria after Nur-ad-Din's death was over the guardianship of his heir, the eleven-year-old boy-king, as-Salih Ismail. The emir of Damascus, Ibn al-Muqaddam, seized the regency first. But the governor of Aleppo, Gümüshtigin, challenged him by securing as-Salih and proclaiming his own regency. Saif-ad-Din of Mosul, the heir's cousin, chose not to interfere yet in the succession conflict, but instead annexed the eastern parts of Nur-ad-Din's kingdom. Salah-ad-Din, unable to move due to a Sicilian threat, wrote to Damascus claiming the regency for himself as a major officer of Nur-ad-Din, and threatening with intervention. To the emirs who reproached him for the implied disloyalty to the Zangid house he replied: "In the interests of Islam and its people we put first and foremost whatever will combine their forces and unite them in one purpose; in the interests of the house of the atabeg we put first and foremost whatever will safeguard its root and its branch. Loyalty can only be the consequence of loyalty. We are in one valley and those who think ill of us are in another."[6] Ibn al-Muqaddam of Damascus appealed to the Franks and Mosul for help but was not assured of any. Consequently, the people of Damascus requested a peaceful surrender to Salah-ad-Din, and he hurried from Egypt with 700 horsemen and occupied the city without resistance. The Franks did not interfere, and the population of Damascus was jubilant. Salah-ad-Din appointed his brother Tughtigin as governor of Damascus and with reinforcements from Egypt advanced northwards to Aleppo.

The struggle over northern Syria lasted for several years as a result of Gümüshtigin's calls for intervention to Mosul, the Franks, and the Ismailian sect (the Assassins). The

[6] Quoted by H.A.R. Gibb, *ibid.*, p. 567.

latter made two unsuccessful attempts on the life of Salah-ad-Din, and provoked him into a siege of their main fortress, Masiaf, in the Nosairi mountains. But soon a treaty was signed by which the Assassins preserved their independence in return for their neutrality. As for the Franks (whose shortcomings and major engagements with Salah-ad-Din will be described separately), their attack on Homs forced Salah-ad-Din to halt his siege of Aleppo temporarily, but the Franks refrained from a major confrontation. Thus Salah-ad-Din captured Homs and Hama, and forced Aleppo to sign an alliance against the Franks in return for his recognition of as-Salih (the boy-king) as his "suzerain." The Franks received in gratitude from Aleppo the release of important prisoners from past battles, one of whom was the famous Reynald of Châtillon, who could be expected to cause trouble to Salah-ad-Din. But with the intervention of Mosul the lines were drawn more clearly. Saif-ad-Din of Mosul sent a large army to challenge Salah-ad-Din's control of Syria, and joined forces with Gümüshtigin of Aleppo. There was a question of legitimacy (over the inheritance of Nur-ad-Din's kingdom) and a question of power to back it, and Salah-ad-Din won both. After a first victory in the field, he renounced his allegiance to as-Salih, and received the formal investiture from the caliph at Bagdad for kingship over Egypt and Syria (May 1175).

The Zangid Saljuqs of Mosul were enraged at this recognition by the caliph of an upstart Kurdish officer, who now enjoyed the support of religious authorities and public opinion in Syria. In 1176, Salah-ad-Din won another decisive battle against Saif-ad-Din and Gümüshtigin near Aleppo, which enabled him to capture the fortresses of Bizaa, Menbij, and Azaz, to the east and north towards the Euphrates River. He could now combine diplomacy with military initiative. A truce was signed including Aleppo, Mosul and its Ortuqid vassals of Mardin and Hisn Kaifa. All prisoners-of-war were returned to Mosul, the castle of Azaz was returned to as-Salih, and the treasury of the defeated armies was distributed among Salah-ad-Din's vic-

CHAPTER 6

torious army. As one historian put it: "His generosity and clemency made an excellent impression."[7] And he continued and elaborated this policy in the years to come. Aleppo, however, remained unconquered behind its heavy walls, and Mosul prepared for another round.

Meanwhile, the Franks were raiding and plundering near Damascus, defeating his brother Turan Shah there in 1175; and later Salah-ad-Din himself was defeated in his imprudent invasion of Jerusalem from Egypt at Montgisard (1177). It gradually became clear to Salah-ad-Din that the precondition for a successful confrontation with the Franks was the complete conquest of Aleppo and Mosul which would give him sufficient manpower while securing his rear in northern Syria. Moreover, experience taught him that the Turks of Syria were much better soldiers than the Egyptians. If Egypt supplied the funds with which greedy Turkish officers could be bought, a solid war machine would be at his disposal. In order to build and consolidate such an empire, it was necessary to sign successive truces with various opponents while dealing with them militarily one by one.

During the years 1179 to 1185, Salah-ad-Din made steady progress toward sultanic solidarity of vast Islamic forces, not without the help of fortunate circumstances. The Ortuqid princes of Mardin and Hisn Kaifa, threatened by the Saljuqid sultan of Asia Minor, Kilij Arslan (who had recently defeated the Byzantines), gave Salah-ad-Din a pretext for direct interference in the politics of Mosul. Since Mosul could not protect them, they voluntarily became a protectorate of Salah-ad-Din. Kilij Arslan was forced to recognize the entire Jazirah (the area of upper Mesopotamia across the Euphrates and to the north of Mosul) as a sphere of influence of Salah-ad-Din. The pressure on Mosul was tightening little by little. Saif-ad-Din of Mosul died in June 1180, and as-Salih of Aleppo died in December 1181. Amidst new confusions over successions, Salah-

[7] S. Runciman, *A History of the Crusades*, Vol. II (Cambridge University Press, 1957), p. 409.

ad-Din conquered the towns of the Jazirah (Edessa, Saruj, Nisibin, Diarbakr) and confronted the forces of Mosul on their home ground. Mosul sought help even from the Franks, but again all the latter could offer was a raid near Damascus. When envoys of the caliph of Bagdad came to mediate, Salah-ad-Din could accuse Mosul of treachery to Jihad by plotting with the Franks, and even with the Saljuqs of Persia against the caliph. He reorganized the Jazirah under his leadership, rewarding his loyal allies with newly conquered towns and fortresses. He now openly claimed his right to control Mosul with the blessing of the caliph. In June 1183 Salah-ad-Din took over Aleppo without a battle, simply by appointing its intimidated emir, Imad-ad-Din, to another province. By 1185, after protecting his rear by a truce with the Franks, he was ready for a final assault on Mosul.

The international position of Salah-ad-Din at this juncture is well summarized by S. Runciman: "His empire now stretched from Cyrenaica to the Tigris. For more than two centuries past there had not been so powerful a Moslem prince. He had the wealth of Egypt behind him. The great cities of Damascus and Aleppo were under his direct government. Around them and north-eastward as far as the walls of Mosul were military fiefs on whose rulers he could rely. The Caliph at Bagdad supported him. Izz ed-Din at Mosul was cowed by him. The Seljuq Sultan in Anatolia sought his friendship, and the Seljuq princes of the East were powerless to oppose him. The Christian Empire of Byzantium was no longer a danger to him. It remained now to suppress the alien intruders whose possession of Palestine and the Syrian littoral was a lasting shame to Islam."[8]

Salah-ad-Din's achievement as a statesman is linked to the effects of the international conflict system by H.A.R. Gibb: "He saw clearly that the weakness of the Muslim body politic, which had permitted the establishment and continued to permit the survival of the crusading states,

[8] Runciman, *ibid.*, p. 435.

was the result of political demoralization. It was against this that he revolted. There was only one way to end it: to restore and revive the political fabric of Islam as a single united empire, not under his own rule, but by restoring the rule of the revealed law, under the direction of the Abbasid Caliphate."[9]

In the previous chapter, three induced functions of the international system were analyzed as results of the efforts of participant units to cope with their international problems:

1) the mutual reinforcement of a spirit of holy wars (crusades and jihads), which produced a pre-national, militant ideology and collective solidarity;

2) a growing tendency to monarchical centralization, induced by the search for extra-feudal resources and by the increased need for a powerful leadership;

3) the appearance of charismatic movements capable of infusing the political system with idealism and adaptational innovations, and threatening thereby the leadership positions of conventional elites.

Salah-ad-Din personified these three functions, as a dedicated champion of Jihad, as an empire builder, and as a charismatic leader. His ideology was well expressed in his dispatches to the caliph: "These three aims—jihad on the path of God, the restraining of actions hurtful to the servants of God, and submission to the caliph of God—are the sole desire of this servitor from the territories in his occupation and his sole gain from the worldly power granted to him. . . . For let him consider, is there anyone else of the governors of Islam whose increase distresses the infidels?"[10] That he succeeded where the Franks had failed is most probably due to the existing congruence between state and religion in medieval Islam, and to the understandable fact that the Franks needed more far-reaching structural changes in order to balance his quantitative achievement.

[9] H.A.R. Gibb, "The Achievement of Saladin," *Bulletin of the John Rylands Library*, Vol. 35 (1952-1953), p. 44.
[10] *Ibid.*, pp. 100-01.

THE COLLAPSE OF THE KINGDOM

Feudal Demoralization

William of Tyre (who became chancellor of Jerusalem in 1175) gives three reasons as to "why the enemy became more powerful against the Christians" at the time of Salah-ad-Din: first, a wicked generation had replaced the religious forefathers and the Lord justly withdraws His favor from people of low morality; second, the older generations of westerners were zealous and enthusiastic, well-trained and capable in warfare against numerically superior armies, while "the people of the East, on the contrary, through long-continued peace, had become enervated; they were unused to the art of war, unfamiliar with the rules of battle, and gloried in their state of inactivity"; third, "In former times almost every city had its own ruler. . . . Those who feared their own allies not less than the Christians could not or would not readily unite to repulse the common danger or arm themselves for our destruction. But now, since God has so willed it, all the Kingdoms adjacent to us have been brought under the power of one man. . . . This Saladin . . . now holds under his control all these kingdoms. . . . From Egypt and the countries adjacent to it, he draws an inestimable supply of the purest gold of the first quality. . . . Other provinces furnish him numberless companies of horsemen and fighters, men thirsty for gold."[11] While the first reason is in the best tradition of the prophets of Israel, and the second describes a low military morale without convincingly explaining it, the third is undoubtedly a clear balance-of-power analysis of the utmost modernity.

As a diplomat and chancellor of Jerusalem, William of Tyre interprets quite secularly the Frankish intervention in favor of as-Salih of Aleppo against Salah-ad-Din: "This was a wise procedure, for any increase of Saladin's power was a cause for suspicion in our eyes and whatever augmented his authority seemed wholly injurious to the good of the Kingdom. For he was a man wise in counsel, valiant in war,

[11] William of Tyre, *History of Deeds Beyond the Sea* (tr. by Babcock and Krey) (Columbia University Press, 1943), pp. 406-07.

CHAPTER 6

and generous beyond measure. All the more, for this very reason, he was distrusted by those of our nobles who had keener foresight.... It seemed wiser to lend aid to the boy king ... not for his own sake, but to encourage him as an adversary against our distrusted rival, Saladin, that the latter's plans might be hindered..."[12]

In the same vein he describes at length the loss of a special opportunity in 1177 to invade Egypt with the aid of the Byzantine fleet (which came to Acre for this purpose) and the crusading forces of Philip, Count of Flanders, who came for ulterior motives and refused to participate. Later William sharply criticizes the failure of the Frankish army to risk an attack upon the invading forces of Salah-ad-Din in the plain of Jezreel in 1183. The terrain was suitable for the heavy Frankish cavalry and all supplies were close at hand. If only the Franks were not divided against themselves, he discloses, they could have destroyed the imprudent invaders.[13] Although the military aspects of this encounter are controversial, the fact of extreme disunity, plottings and counterplottings, in the highest echelons of the Kingdom is indisputable. In fact, the demoralization of the Franks coincided with the formation of Salah-ad-Din's empire.

If it was not for lack of understanding of balance-of-power strategies that the Franks failed to countervail the achievements of Salah-ad-Din, the question arises as to what factors beyond their control, or what cultural compulsions stood in their way. We have already examined the structural effects of the international conflict system upon both the Christian and Islamic societies. We have noted the limits of feudal capacity to cope with institutionally unanticipated situations. There is no doubt that the Jerusalemite feudalism operated "with a difference," and that it responded to its international problems with adaptational innovations. The unfolding of its weaknesses in the face of Salah-ad-Din's revolution, however, discloses how insuffi-

[12] *Ibid.*, pp. 405-06.   [13] *Ibid.*, p. 497.

cient and inadequate these innovations were. If the crusaders did not have a sufficiently large urban population upon which they could rely for defense while their mobile army took more daring initiatives in the field, it was because the feudal aristocracy would not encourage political autonomy of urban communities with strong militias. If they often engaged in pillaging raids and broke truces, it was because they needed more supplies and money than could be raised from regular revenues. If their knightly army was small, it was because their agricultural territory was small and impoverished. For lack of income they could not employ as many mercenaries as they needed. And for lack of understanding they did not maximize the growth of the religio-military orders, which provided them with an inexpensive standing army, a suitable form of colonization, and the most dedicated element to the idea of the Holy Land. In other words: the feudal aristocracy trusted in conventional feudal structure.

The internal strife accompanying the events to be presently described was quite normal from a feudal point of view. There was nothing unusual about the behavior of the contending parties regarding leadership or group interests in comparison to feudal European principalities under similar dynastic circumstances. The only non-typical circumstance was the international crisis of the Kingdom. The feudal aristocracy of Jerusalem was ready to face it, but on its own terms.

The immediate issue in Jerusalem after Amalric's death was over the bailliage (regency) and the problem of hereditary royal continuity. The legitimate heir, Baldwin IV, was thirteen years old and a leper. Although he was crowned, it was obvious that somone else would have to rule on his behalf. But who? And who should arrange for the marriage of his sister Sibyl, so that a future king might be born? From the viewpoint of the native barons, it was necessary to restore the balance of power between themselves and the monarch, which had been disturbed during the authoritarian reign of Amalric. They had evidence that the seneschal,

CHAPTER 6

Miles of Plancy, "was secretly taking steps to seize the royal power."[14] His influence in the Kingdom increased rapidly due to his earlier friendship with Amalric and his lordship over the fief of Transjordan. In the eyes of the native barons he was an upstart newcomer from Europe with dangerous authoritarian tendencies. The barons' candidate for the regency was Raymond III of Tripoli, a native count, a cousin of Amalric, and the lord of Galilee by a recent marriage. But in the royal house there was reason to suspect that Raymond, who did not hold Tripoli as a vassal county of the king, could have ambitions of inheriting the crown of Jerusalem, and, at any rate, would not act in the best interests of the dynasty. At a first hearing Raymond's request for the regency was left undecided. A short while later Miles of Plancy was murdered in the streets of Acre. Then the High Court assembled in full, and Raymond was invested with the regency.[15]

This ominous beginning of internal conflict soon widened into fundamental differences on foreign policy. Salah-ad-Din was just starting his bid for the annexation of northern Syria, and Raymond's intervention at Homs was short and indecisive. In 1175 he surprisingly accepted a truce with Salah-ad-Din, who needed a free hand to deal effectively with Saif-ad-Din of Mosul. William of Tyre criticized the constable, Humphrey of Toron, for mediating this truce: "His action was decidedly detrimental to our interests, for thus this prince who should have been resisted to the utmost, lest his insolence toward us increase with his power, won our good will . . ."[16] When in the following year the Franks broke the truce (due to second thoughts?) and defeated the militia of Damascus, it was too late, for Salah-ad-Din had already won a great victory in the north, and hurried south to drive the Franks away. This shortsighted avoidance of risk by Raymond cannot be easily understood. There is, however, a widely accepted view that Raymond represented the outlook of the old-guard native

[14] *Ibid.*, p. 402.   [15] *Ibid.*, pp. 399-402.
[16] *Ibid.*, p. 410.

barons, partly orientalized, interested in establishing a *modus vivendi* with their Moslem neighbors, as against the adventurous "newcomers," eager for personal gain through any change in the status quo. But the cleavage was actually more complex.

Just as the self-assertive baronial aristocracy insisted on its right (formerly a duty) to give counsel, or, in the absence of a strong monarch, to rule through the semi-parliamentary High Court, so the royal family joined hands with dissenting or dissatisfied elements to curb baronial power, to assert dynastic interests, and to assure monarchical leadership. Thus the unscrupulous "plottings" of Baldwin's mother, Agnes, and his sister, Sibyl, with the patriarch and with Reynald of Châtillon and Joscelin of Edessa (the former having just returned from sixteen years in Moslem captivity and thirsty for action, and the latter a "Count without a county"),[17] and, later, with personal enemies of Raymond such as Gerard of Ridfort,[18] and the Lusignan brothers. All such ties had to do with internal struggles, no less than with foreign policy differences. The division of the religio-military orders is also not wholly explainable in terms of differences on foreign policy. The Hospitallers supported Raymond (due to vested interests in Tripoli?), while the Templars aligned themselves with the aggressive party. In Amalric's time it had been the Hospitallers who went along with the adventures in Egypt, while the Templars were in favor of keeping the defensive treaty with the Fatimids. The Orders were encroaching upon the prerogatives of the Church (to the point that sharp warnings had even come from their "suzerain," the Pope) and yet the patriarch and some higher clerics were in the royal camp with the Templars, while most of the bishops were in the moderate baronial camp. As to the young but sick king, he

[17] S. Runciman (*ibid.*, p. 405).
[18] An errant knight formerly in Tripoli. Raymond promised him a fief through marriage and then renounced it and gave the prize to a rich Italian merchant. Gerard joined the Templars and became their Master, which, by the way, illustrates how status in the Orders depended on achievement rather than property or lineage.

CHAPTER 6

tried to strike a middle course between the parties, while being influenced intermittently by both extremities.

The year 1177 was troublesome but it ended on a note of hope for Jerusalem. Baldwin IV, in spite of his illness, assumed the royal power when he reached sixteen, and Raymond relinquished the regency. Previously that year, the king and the High Court had provided for the future of the dynasty by inviting William of Montferrat ("Longsword") from France to marry Sibyl and serve as regent. With the marriage the princess received the county of Jaffa and Askalon as dowry. But William died within a year, and his only contribution was a newborn heir for the Kingdom (the future Baldwin V), which reopened the problem of the regency and the marriage of Sibyl. The next candidate for regency was Count Philip of Flanders who came with a strong detachment of knights (following the tradition of his father, the private crusader, Count Thierry). New hopes were associated with this visit, as a Byzantine fleet was waiting for him at Acre to make a joint invasion of Egypt (according to a previous treaty with King Amalric). But, overestimating his bargaining position, Philip demanded that two young sons of an insignificant vassal of his should marry the princesses Sibyl and Isabel (Amalric's daughter by Maria the Byzantine). This was opposed mainly by the barons, who felt responsible for future leadership and saw through Philip's designs for absentee influence in Jerusalem. While this "diplomacy" was going on, Salah-ad-Din was making his own preparations in Egypt. After the Byzantine fleet had left, disgusted with the Frankish inability to abide by the plan to attack Egypt, and as the Count of Flandres moved northward to aid Tripoli and Antioch in minor campaigns, Salah-ad-Din invaded the Kingdom of Jerusalem from the south. This sudden attack found the Franks unprepared. As Baldwin marched to Askalon with 500 knights, the Egyptian army advanced directly towards Jerusalem, ravaging the countryside, burning the deserted city of Ramlah, and causing panic even behind the defenseless walls of Jerusalem. At this point

THE COLLAPSE OF THE KINGDOM

Baldwin was locked up in Askalon and summoned the rest of the army to him. The Templars were ordered to abandon their fortress in Gaza and join the force in Askalon. The Franks had no choice but to risk a swift counterattack. They caught the over-confident Egyptian camp by surprise at Montgisard and routed it completely. Salah-ad-Din himself narrowly escaped. His entire expedition fled, leaving behind weapons and equipment.[19]

The victory of Montgisard did not result in any serious regaining of initiative by the Franks. Considering that earlier that year, before the destruction of Salah-ad-Din's army, they had been about to invade Egypt, their present inactivity indicates either extreme weakness in manpower or lack of leadership. They had two alternatives: one, to follow up their victory into Egypt with the knowledge that Damascene forces were tied up with Aleppo; second, to coordinate with Aleppo an attack on Damascus while Salah-ad-Din's Egyptian army was reduced to almost nonexistence. Instead, the Franks embarked on building fortifications on the frontier with Damascus. This gave Salah-ad-Din time to reorganize his forces, and when, in 1179, the Franks attempted pillaging raids across the frontier, they suffered two defeats in which they lost their constable and the Master of the Temple. Then Salah-ad-Din succeeded in destroying the newly built castle at Jacob's Ford, putting all the defenders to death. Previously, he had prepared an Egyptian fleet which was now able to perform a successful raid on Acre. At this point King Baldwin sent messengers

[19] It is interesting to note here William of Tyre's remark (*ibid.*, p. 434) on the absence of any other forces except Jerusalem's in this victory: "For if the count of Flandres, the prince of Antioch, the Count of Tripoli . . . had participated in this victory brought about by divine grace, they would not have hesitated to think, 'Our hand is high, and the Lord hath not done all this.' For heedless and inconsiderate persons are wont to creep in thus when all is prosperous." It seems that the archbishop was displaying, in addition to piety, his resentment of the recent noncooperation of these forces, and their futile siege of Harim in the north. He does not point out, however, that with these dissenting forces at hand Egypt could now be attacked.

CHAPTER 6

to Salah-ad-Din to negotiate a truce. Salah-ad-Din, interested in a free hand for pursuing his goals in the Jazirah, and also because of rainless years and famine in the region, agreed immediately. In May 1180 a two-year truce "on land and sea" was signed.[20]

The respite on the foreign front marked the exacerbation of internal intrigues. One of the "newcomers," Amalric of Lusignan, was the lover of Agnes and became the constable after the death of Humphrey of Toron. He and Agnes had a "solution" to the problem of regency and the dynasty. His young brother, Gui, should come from France to marry Sibyl. In this way Agnes expected to prevent the promised marriage of Sibyl to Baldwin of Ibelin, who sided with the native baronial party, and Amalric hoped to create a promising career for his brother. To the dismay of the barons, King Baldwin yielded to family pressure and gave his consent. At this point Raymond of Tripoli with Bohemond III of Antioch entered the Kingdom with their armies, in an effort to threaten the marriage. But the king reacted by marrying Sibyl and Gui immediately, thus presenting the opposition with an established fact (April 1180).

Now the conflict between the court family and the native barons turned into a bitter and continuous struggle for power, with the future crown of Jerusalem at stake. By the end of 1180 another favorite of Agnes', Heraclius, Archbishop of Caesarea, was "elected" to the key position of the patriarchate, despite his bad reputation. The more qualified candidate and scholar, William of Tyre, was later excommunicated by Heraclius on some trivial pretext, and

[20] William of Tyre (*ibid.*, p. 447) recognizes that Salah-ad-Din signed the truce not because "he had any reason to fear our forces, which he had so often defeated during the past year," and he gives the drought as the reason. Then he makes the following interesting comment: "The conditions were somewhat humiliating to us, for the truce was concluded on equal terms, with no reservations of importance on our part, a thing which is said never to have happened before." This change of status which the Moslems now imposed and the Franks were ready to accept was symbolic of the revolution in the balance of power that was affecting the relative morale of both sides.

THE COLLAPSE OF THE KINGDOM

had to leave the country for Rome to defend himself. Meanwhile, Reynald of Châtillon, who acquired the lordship of Transjordan by marriage, broke the truce with Salah-ad-Din by pillaging a big Moslem caravan on the Damascus-Mecca road (1181). Salah-ad-Din requested reparations but Reynald defied even King Baldwin on this matter. A series of Moslem retaliations started. First, hundreds of Christian pilgrims were captured near Egypt, then villages were sacked and crops devastated in Galilee. The fortress of Habis Jaldak in Transjordan was sieged and conquered, and finally in 1182, Beirut was besieged by combined land and sea operations. Earlier in 1182, when Raymond of Tripoli had tried to reenter his barony of Galilee, King Baldwin, who was then under the complete sway of the court family party, threatened to meet him with force. But the native barons, closing ranks, mediated between them and a civil clash was prevented. It was probably the mounting foreign dangers which postponed the internal conflict in Jerusalem. Mosul and Aleppo pleaded with the Franks to divert Salah-ad-Din's offensive in the Jazirah by attacking Damascus. They promised money, Banyas, and Habis Jaldak in return, but the supreme interest of the Franks alone would have been enough to prompt interference. King Baldwin and Raymond made raids up to the suburbs of Damascus, recapturing Habis Jaldak; but aside from much pillaging, they accomplished nothing. Plans were made for additional campaigns, but Baldwin's leprosy got worse and confined him to bed. The family court party persuaded him to appoint Gui of Lusignan as regent, a development which the barons had long feared. Meanwhile, Reynald of Châtillon began a private war of his own, and a very daring one. He built a little fleet and carried the galleys to the gulf of Ailat at the Red Sea. From there they sailed along the Arabian coast, pillaging merchant ships and caravans from Egypt and the Indian Ocean. They burnt ports as far as Mecca and sank a pilgrim ship. Finally, Salah-ad-Din's brother in Egypt, al-Adil, succeeded in destroying the "young navy" of Reynald to the last boat.

CHAPTER 6

But Salah-ad-Din continued annexing the cities of the Jazirah, and in 1183 he entered Aleppo and Harim (see above). His empire now enveloped the crusading principalities.

The Kingdom of Jerusalem anticipated a major invasion and declared a state of emergency. A step unprecedented in feudalism was taken when a general tax (based on percentage from property or income) was levied and the entire population was put on the alert. The military confrontation took place at the end of the summer of 1183. Salah-ad-Din crossed the Jordan with his reinforced army and encamped deep in the valley of Jezreel. Gui of Lusignan summoned all the forces of the Kingdom, including the religio-military orders and some minor visiting crusaders. The two large armies faced each other for several days. The "hot heads," like Reynald of Châtillon, advised a major showdown. The barons advised Gui not to risk an all-out assault, either because of sound tactical considerations or because they feared that the credit for victory would assure Gui of lasting leadership, if not the crown of the dying king. Undoubtedly, losing the battle would expose the entire kingdom to Salah-ad-Din, while confronting him passively would immobilize him and ultimately force him to withdraw.[21] Gui hesitated and Salah-ad-Din withdrew, apparently because he had failed to lure the Franks out of their defensive formation.

For Gui of Lusignan the consequences were disastrous. He lost face with the army, and he got into arguments with King Baldwin. The baronial party was gaining the ascendance, spreading insinuating rumors about Gui's intentions with respect to the crown. Baldwin assembled the High Court, deposed Gui from the regency, and hurriedly crowned his six-year-old nephew (Baldwin V, son of Sibyl by her previous marriage). The regency went again to Raymond of Tripoli (1183).

---

[21] For a detailed analysis of the tactical aspects of this battle and similar situations see R. C. Smail, *Crusading Warfare* (Cambridge University Press, 1956), pp. 150-56.

THE COLLAPSE OF THE KINGDOM

Gui revolted by repudiating his allegiance to the king and fortified himself in Askalon. Realizing that if anything happened to the child-king, Gui could reclaim the regency as Sibyl's husband, the barons arranged for the stepsister of Baldwin IV, Princess Isabel, to marry the young Humphrey of Toron, so that he could legitimately qualify for the regency or the crown. Meanwhile, King Baldwin IV had a chance to lead one more battle (from a litter) against Salah-ad-Din, before he died. That was when Salah-ad-Din besieged the fortress of Kerak where the marriage of Isabel and Humphrey took place.

The feudal rebellion of Gui went on through 1185, as Baldwin IV made his will. It specified that Raymond would remain regent, and if the child-king should die before the age of ten, the matter of the crown should be arbitrated by the Pope, the Emperor, and the kings of France and England. Joscelin of Courtenay (of the family court party) got the personal guardianship of the child-king. Baldwin IV died in March 1185.

O' God, The Heathen Came Into Thine Inheritance

Since the early successes of Salah-ad-Din, the Franks had been desperately seeking help from Europe—preferably a large crusade—but to no avail. After 1176, the balancing power of the Byzantine empire in northern Syria disappeared, and a few years after the death of Manuel (1180) it declined rapidly, and even sought the favor of Salah-ad-Din. In 1183, after Salah-ad-Din's invasion and the deposition of Gui, an impressive delegation was sent to Europe: the Patriarch Heraclius, the Master of the Templars, Arnold of Toroga, and the Master of the Hospitallers, Roger of Les Moulins. For two years they searched Europe in vain for reinforcements. King Henry II of England considered the idea of a crusade for a while, but eventually dropped it and instead contributed a large sum of money for the recruitment of mercenaries. But Jerusalem needed "a prince that needeth money, not money that needeth a prince."

CHAPTER 6

In 1185 Raymond, with the approval of the High Court, signed a four-year truce with Salah-ad-Din. The latter again needed it in order to be free to act against Izz-ad-Din of Mosul, who threatened to start a secession in the Jazirah; and the Franks were determined to stay on the defensive until the arrival of another crusade. The country was damaged by the intense hostilities of the past years, accompanied by large-scale devastation of fields and properties (a result of the increasing amount of battles in Jerusalem's territory), and further impoverishment resulted from a drought that year. With the truce, trade was renewed and famine was avoided. Yet by the beginning of 1186, Salah-ad-Din had succeeded in cowing Mosul into definite vassaldom, and was free to contemplate his situation with the Franks. He could not predict, however, that during that year the Franks would plunge into a civil war, and would violate the truce, giving him a cause for war.

In the summer of 1186 the child-king, Baldwin V, died suddenly (could it have been due to willful neglect on the part of his guardian, Joscelin, an intimate ally of Agnes and the Lusignans?). The family court party was much better prepared for the occasion than Raymond and the barons. Joscelin, after deceiving Raymond on the burial arrangements, sent forces to occupy Tyre and Beirut, while he himself controlled Acre, and proclaimed Sibyl as Queen. At Joscelin's request, the Templars carried the king's body to Jerusalem, while Sibyl with her rebel husband Gui and Reynald of Châtillon occupied Jerusalem. There was the Patriarch Heraclius ready to perform a coronation, and Raymond's enemy, the Master of the Templars, Gerard of Ridfort, eager to back the "revolution." All of these (except the Master of the Hospitallers) were about to violate their prior oaths to abide by the arbitration of the Pope and the kings of Europe. When Raymond learned of the conspiracy he summoned the High Court to Nablus (Balian of Ibelin's estate), and the forces of the native barons started emergency consultations. But the rebels felt strong enough to proceed with their legally untenable *fait accompli*. The patriarch crowned Sibyl, and she placed a second crown on the head of Gui, who was to be the actual king. The barons at Nablus decided to counteract first legalistically by crowning Isabel and Humphrey, and then by force. They all counted on Salah-ad-Din to honor the truce while Jerusalem settled its affairs in a civil war. At this point Humphrey lost heart and fled to Jerusalem, where he paid homage to Gui. With this defection the barons considered their battle lost. One by one they offered submission to Gui, all except Baldwin of Ibelin (whom Sibyl betrayed) and Raymond, who, as legal regent, renounced allegiance to the usurper king and retired to Tiberias. Gui prepared his troops for a final showdown with Raymond at Tiberias. But Raymond, who felt cheated not only of his legitimate regency but also of a possible crown, sent for help to— Salah-ad-Din. The latter was delighted to dispatch some troops to Tiberias and promised more. Bohemond of Antioch was also in full sympathy with Raymond.

Now it was Reynald of Châtillon's turn to make his typical contribution to the crisis. He broke the truce with Salah-ad-Din by attacking a rich caravan on the road from Egypt to Damascus, slaying its guards and taking an enormous booty. Salah-ad-Din was still willing to respect the truce, providing that his losses were repaired, but Gui was in no position to force Reynald to yield anything. At this point Salah-ad-Din proclaimed the Jihad against Jerusalem.

This was early in 1187. While Salah-ad-Din prepared for war, Balian of Ibelin tried to mediate between Gui and Raymond. Emissaries were sent back and forth to try and negotiate a compromise. Raymond was still intransigent, relying on his separate treaty with Salah-ad-Din. When the latter asked permission for the passing of a reconnaisance expedition through Galilee, Raymond concurred, with the stipulation that they enter the country at sunrise, leave before dark, and refrain from attacking inhabited places. At the same time, torn as he was between self-defense and loyalty to his fellow Christians, Raymond informed the Franks of what was coming. The result of this doubtful deal

CHAPTER 6

was a brief encounter near Nazareth between 7,000 Moslems and a hurriedly organized company of Templars and other knights. The latter were all slain, including the Master of the Hospitallers. The Master of the Templars, Gerard, who invoked the rash attack, was among the few wounded fugitives. Only after this shameful disaster did Raymond and Gui come to terms; Raymond submitted homage to Gui in Jerusalem. Thus the unification of the Kingdom was achieved in the last moment before its downfall. But, as one historian has put it, "ill-feeling between the two parties still smoldered under the surface of apparent harmony."[22]

While it must not be stressed too strongly, there is ample reason to suppose that Salah-ad-Din did not expect too much of the forthcoming battle of Hittin. His previous experiences in major confrontations with the total Frankish army *on its own territory* were not too promising. In 1177 he had been severely defeated on the southern coast by the small army of Baldwin IV. In two other major invasions (1182 and 1183) the Franks had employed their traditional tactics of avoiding premature all-out combats which could result in annihilation of their scarce manpower. They consistently preserved their formation near a base well-supplied with water, and could not be lured into false retreats (the traditional Turkish tactic, aimed at separating the cavalry from the foot soldiers who shielded the horses) unless afforded an opportunity to charge with maximum impact upon an imprudent enemy. Moreover, as Salah-ad-Din and the Franks knew very well, an invading army could not stay indefinitely in the field, immobilized by a matching defense army, since its supplies could be exhausted and its formation sidetracked in foraging efforts. There was also the problem of the seasonal discharge of troops at the end of summer, when they had to return to their estates to attend to other business. Salah-ad-Din, in fact, had not yet conquered a single city of the Franks, and his sieges of

---

[22] Marshall W. Baldwin, in Setton and Baldwin, *ibid.*, p. 608. See also Baldwin, *Raymond III of Tripolis and the Fall of Jerusalem, 1140-1187* (Princeton University Press, 1936).

Kerak could only inform him of how unrewarding such attempts were. His limited, although significant, accomplishments in invading Frankish territory so far were destructive raids which impoverished the Kingdom's means of subsistence. If he was to attempt a liquidation of the Kingdom, his reasonable course of action would be to attract the bulk of the Frankish army into a remote section of the frontier (such as Kerak) while striking with another strong army at its heart. But, despite his vast resources in manpower, he did not gather a much larger army for Hittin than the Franks had. Thus it must not be assumed that Salah-ad-Din could count on the Franks to be easily lured into his chosen terrain near Tiberias rather than waiting for him to be lured into the interior and opposing him at a place advantageous to them, as they had usually done in the past.[23]

Yet the unexpected was going to happen. At the end of June 1187 Salah-ad-Din crossed the Jordan south of Lake Kineret and attacked Tiberias, while occupying positions on the surrounding hills. The army of Jerusalem began to gather in the village of Saffuriyah, northwest of Nazareth, while King Gui held a counsel at Acre. Numerically the forces were about equal—roughly 20,000 on each side. The Moslems were as usual stronger in light cavalry of archers, and the Franks had 1,200 heavily armed knights (half of whom were members of the religio-military orders), 3,000-4,000 light cavalry of the native Turcopoles, a substantial number of mounted bowmen, and nearly 10,000 foot soldiers. The tactical conditions of the terrain were very clear: the area between the Frankish camp and the lake (where the Moslems were) was devoid of water and the hills were more conducive to light cavalry. The Franks could either contest the position of the Moslems near the lake, risking thereby a battle in a place chosen by Salah-ad-Din for obvious reasons, or they could stay at the well-supplied Saffuriyah on the safe assumption that if the invading army

[23] For systematic military analysis of these considerations, see R. C. Smail, *ibid.*, pp. 138-203, with special reference to the battle of Hittin. See also M. W. Baldwin, *Raymond of Tripoli*, Ch. VI.

CHAPTER 6

would not move to the interior it would have to retreat as usual of its own accord at the end of the fighting season. If, however, the Moslems insisted on combat, they would have to leave their water supply, and the Frankish army would have its best chance and a superior terrain, right where it camped. Time was, then, on the side of the Franks, since Salah-ad-Din had revealed his intentions. If he wanted more than Tiberias he would have to take new and daring initiatives. In fact, he could not even hope to hold Tiberias very long unless he moved into the disadvantageous interior. All this was generally agreed at the Frankish council, where Raymond was the chief speaker. He insisted on applying the same tactics which had forced Salah-ad-Din's retreat in 1183. Although Tiberias was Raymond's city, and his wife was besieged there, he realized that an attempt to save them would mean defeat and loss of the Kingdom. Crossing the waterless area in the heavy heat of July would substantially reduce the efficiency of the army. Besides, Tiberias could be recovered later, and his wife could be released by ransom. If anyone was to venture a crossing and an attack, let it be Salah-ad-Din. The majority of the barons agreed and so it was decided. But ill-feelings still smoldered beneath a surface of apparent harmony.

Immediately after the war council made its decision, Gerard of Ridfort, Master of the Templars, went to King Gui and asked, "Sire, are you going to trust a traitor?"[24] Gerard was trying to convince Gui that the barons were trying to trick him again (as in 1183), that they intended to disgrace him if he behaved "cowardly." The Templars would lose faith in him. Apparently Gerard was not alone in this opinion. Reynald of Châtillon and other adventurers were also disappointed in the decision taken on that evening. Gui vacillated in a dilemma. He was convinced one way at the council, and now he was convinced the other way. Impulsively he took matters into his own hands and ordered the march on Tiberias. Evidently, the king as com-

[24] Quoted by Runciman, *ibid.*, p. 456.

mander-in-chief of the army could reverse his council's decisions.

What ensued was precisely what Raymond had predicted. The military historian R. C. Smail outlines the events of Hittin as follows: "Its significant episodes were first, the Christian decision to relieve Tiberias; second, the Muslims' success in compelling the Franks to halt and bivouac in waterless country between Saffuriya and Tiberias; third, the collapse and destruction of the Christian army on the following morning."[25] The dramatic battle of Hittin, where a miserably thirsty army which had been forced to halt overnight without water, was cut to pieces in the morning, and the subsequent landslide conquest of the Kingdom of Jerusalem (except for Tyre and a few dispersed fortresses) has been so extensively described and analyzed from various vantage points that another detailed attempt is hardly necessary.[26]

Yet one general remark (without confidence that it too has not been made before) seems most relevant in the context of this study. Although the Frankish military breakdown at Hittin was an accident, the destruction of the feudal Kingdom of Jerusalem was not. This has been the cumulative thesis throughout the previous chapters and it will be summarized in the concluding chapter. In essence this thesis may be formulated as follows: the transplanted Kingdom of Jerusalem ultimately behaved as though it was still within the international system of European feudalism, while the different international system, which Jerusalem itself had helped to form, required a changed society and another type of state as a *sine qua non* for survival. One cogent factual argument for this explanation is the failure of even the armies of England and France in the Third Crusade (and the later crusades of the 13th century) to revive the Kingdom of Jerusalem as a viable feudal

---

[25] R. C. Smail, *ibid.*, p. 191.
[26] In addition to the sources mentioned here, see Charles Oman, *A History of the Art of War in the Middle Ages*, 2 vols. (Burt Franklin, 1953).

CHAPTER 6

entity encircled by a Moslem empire. The survival of littoral petty feudal principalities in Acre, Tripoli, and Antioch until 1291 was really a continued testimony to institutional lag in a changing international system. Europe itself was a changed society by then, but it was not prepared (psychologically or militarily) to contest with Islam the control of the Holy Land.[27]

When Salah-ad-Din entered Jerusalem on October 2, 1187, he did not revenge the massacre of the First Crusade on July 5, 1099. Indeed, he had already executed all the prisoners from the religio-military orders at his victorious camp in Hittin, and he had slain Reynald of Châtillon with his own sword, but that was a special reckoning with "war criminals." His subsequent policy was to expedite the surrender of all pockets of resistance without war before the enemy could recover from the shock of defeat. He, therefore, conducted himself as the most merciful and generous king ever known to a conquered people. And, it may not all have been shrewd propaganda; it could well be that Salah-ad-Din was a humane statesman. Prisoners such as King Gui and Gerard, the Master of the Templars, were used to obtain the surrender of Askalon and Gaza. The people of Acre and Jerusalem were permitted to leave by the thousands with and without ransom. The holy places were respected, and Greek Orthodox natives were allowed immediate control over them. Patriarch Heraclius left Jerusalem honorably with all the Church's funds at his disposal, and so did the officers of the Temple and Hospital. Three large caravans of refugees moved northward along the coast: one headed by the Templars, another by the Hospitallers, and the third by Balian and the patriarch.

[27] When a British historian wrote an unsigned description of General Allenby's conquest of Jerusalem in 1917, he meant it to be, symbolically, "the final anonymous continuation of William of Tyre" (John L. La Monte, "Some Problems in Crusading Historiography," *Speculum*, XV [1940], 60). On the 13th-century crusading principality, see La Monte, "From Crusader Kingdom to Commercial Colony," *Bulletin of the Polish Institute of Arts and Sciences in America*, Vol. III (January 1945), 288-99.

They moved towards Tyre, Tripoli, and Antioch, which became overcrowded with refugees. Antioch and Tripoli lost most of their lands and fortresses. But the concentration of Franks in the impregnable city of Tyre was underestimated by Salah-ad-Din. It was soon to become the rallying point for a formidable Frankish resurgence before the advent of the Third Crusade.

Meanwhile, two incompatible religious outcries were addressed to God and his peoples about the fate of the Holy City of Jerusalem. The Pope in Rome, shocked by the Christian calamity and hoping for another Crusade, wrote to the kings and princes of Europe: "O' God, the heathen came into thine inheritance, the Holy Temple have they defiled, they have laid Jerusalem in heaps . . ."[28] In Jerusalem the *qadi* of Damascus, Ibn az-Zaki, preaching a *khutba* (Friday sermon) in the presence of Salah-ad-Din, said: "Praise be unto God by whose aid Islam hath been exalted and by whose might polytheism hath been humbled. . . . God is pleased with your conduct . . . in as much as He rendered it easy for your hands to recover this strayed camel [Jerusalem] from the possession of a misguided people, and bring it back to the fold of Islam, after it had been abused by the polytheists for nearly one hundred years. . . ."[29]

[28] Quoted by G. A. Campbell, *ibid.*, p. 108.
[29] Quoted by M. E. Bertsch, "Counter-Crusade: A Study of Twelfth Century Jihad in Syria and Palestine" (unpublished Ph.D. dissertation; University of Michigan, 1950).

Conclusions

My conclusion will be confined to generalizations based on this particular case study, resting completely on its experimental worth. The temptation to graft these generalizations onto an existing theory of social change may result in prejudicing the findings from the case itself without benefitting much the recipient theory. A case study cannot establish or disprove a theory. It can only contribute empirical generalizations suggesting some theoretical import. Let this conclusion, therefore, stand on its own incompleteness for future reevaluation of its relevance.

Social Structure and Change in an Inter-societal Context

In the case of the feudal Kingdom of Jerusalem, history itself kept social structure constant while varying the inter-societal factor. The fact that it was a case of transplantation resulting in a changed relationship with other societies does not limit its experimental value to transplantation. For a society does not have to migrate in order to find itself operating in a definitely changed inter-societal relationship. Many contemporary studies have dealt with national problems introduced by technological leads or lags between internationally related societies. As pointed out earlier, when politically organized societies are viewed as interlocked units impinging upon one another, any internal change in one social system (technological, economic, demographic, organizational, ideological, etc.) which has a balance-changing significance, might induce countervailing efforts in the affected units of the conflict system. Thus, for the analysis of

CONCLUSIONS

social change, related social systems cannot be considered as environmental constants to one another, but as changing variables in a unified framework. It also follows that social structures as such normally contain institutional patterns oriented toward interaction with other societies. We have referred to the observable consequences of such interactions as induced functions. This type of exogenous influence should be distinguished from the one obtained by cultural contact and the ensuing process of diffusion of cultural elements. The latter is essentially a process by which some *solutions to problems* are communicated from one system to another (e.g. a tool) while the former involves the *introduction of problems* (often critical ones) through political interaction, and the ensuing social development in response.

The case in question illustrates that quite clearly. It corresponds in principle to the requirements of controlled experiments in which a causal connection is sought between a changing independent variable (inter-societal system) and a dependent variable (social structure) while other comparable variables are being controlled. We have observed the differences between the two successive modes of international existence of a feudal society, and the resulting modifications of it. The vitality and stability of feudal institutions in the European inter-societal system (the "control groups" for the period in question) was contrasted with the chronic crisis and peculiarities of the feudal Kingdom of Jerusalem in the Middle East. Its innovations in social organization (especially the religio-military orders) were found unique in feudalism and positively related to the security needs of Jerusalem. On the other hand, the collapse of the Kingdom was associated with regressive feudal decentralization, and with the problem of manpower which grew beyond the reach of feudal organization.

Finally it was observed that the inter-societal system itself reflected, in its historical turning points, the relative capacity of conflicting societies to respond with structural changes to one another and to affect one another's social organization. The Islamic Jihad as a counter-Crusade, the political unification under charismatic heroes and empire builders, and the religious and moral rearmament of the urban population were induced processes which paralleled those of the crusaders' society.

Stratification and Functions of Political Leadership

Stratification systems are usually analyzed by concepts of internal social structure such as "relations of production," or "functional importance and scarcity of personnel" associated with motivated mobility or immobility. It would appear, at first sight, that with respect to inter-societal relations it is the vested interests of ruling classes or the political culture of domestic groups which shape international relations rather than the other way around. Our case, however, suggests a dialectical connection between international relations and stratification.

First, we have referred to Marc Bloch's treatment of the emergence of vassalage and serfdom as adaptational innovations in the *protective function* of communities at a time when neither the state nor kinship organization provided adequate protection. Since functional importance in satisfying the need for *security* facilitated the ascendance of the knightly class, it follows that feudalism as a form of social organization cannot be fully explained without reference to inter-societal relations. Thus the feudal ruling class gained control over the regulation of man-to-man relations by virtue of its capacity to regulate community-to-community relations. Its monopoly over the means of warfare was transformed into control of the means of production and of social institutions at large.

Second, as a stable stratification system within a network of decentralized states, it rested on the personal solidarity of groups of warriors in collective defense of their properties, these being identical with the territory of the state. In other words, a feudal army was not an instrument in the hands of a class-transcending central authority, but rather a ruling class in action. However, as the case of Jerusalem in-

CONCLUSIONS

dicates, as soon as feudalism had to operate in a different international setting (i.e., in changed relationships with other societies) the preservation of its traditional stratification became problematic. New groupings (with functional importance to security) began challenging the leadership positions of the conventional aristocracy. We have observed how the religio-military orders combined qualities, claims, and obligations of both the secular and ecclesiastic establishments, thus posing as a church-in-arms or a Godly army. Since they could be used not only against the enemy but also as a central tool to discipline feudal rebels, they suggested the possibility of a viable monarchy independent of the institution of vassalage. But the self-conscious and frightened feudal elites, failing to discharge their customary protective functions, reacted with conservative legislation (the assises) to confirm and systematize purely feudal customs, shielding the knightly class from a possible reorganization of the state. On the other hand, the kings, representing leadership on the inter-societal plane, strove for better security through a centralized monarchy, which could not be attained without overcoming the feudo-vassalic monopoly over the means of warfare.

Finally, as the international system on the Moslem side ceased to consist of fragmented units and changed into an integrated empire, Jerusalemite feudalism faced its dilemma between centralization (based on extra-feudal resources and manpower) and destruction.

To what extent can this finding be generalized? Considering the widely accepted view that socio-economic factors normally shape and reshape stratification systems, one would have to counter this by presenting much historical evidence for the extreme capacity of power elites to preserve a given structure of privileges so long as they can meet their political leadership functions on the international plane. But that is beyond the scope of this study. It does seem, however, that relations between politically organized societies play a greater role with respect to the shaping of stratification than is commonly believed.

CHAPTER 7

Fusion of Divergent Social Roles as a Form of Social Change

The process by which two divergent roles in society fuse or blend into one appears contrary to the much-observed process of differentiation or specialization. The only possible connection between these two processes would be dialectical. If, as Durkheim has shown, specialization leads to "organic solidarity" due to greater interdependence of mutually complementary roles, so can an innovative combination of role elements from two separate social positions contribute to social integration by mutual reinforcement. The historical phenomenon exemplified by the special synthesis of the knight and monk roles in the feudal Kingdom of Jerusalem is probably not as unique as it appears. One is tempted to make analogies (*mutatis mutandis*) with such modern phenomena as the fusion of the salaried-managerial role with the capitalist-entrepreneurial role; the blending of the priest, minister, or rabbi with the community-administrator role; the fusion of the military leadership role with the political-ideological leadership role in many societies. One can ask, what are the conditions under which such fusions take place? But this will take us too far afield. We shall, therefore, characterize only the role fusion of the religio-military orders, leaving the question of general applicability open.

We have characterized at length (in Chapters Three and Five) the movement of fighting monks in Jerusalem. Thus it is only necessary to recapitulate here some of its features which seem relevant for the construction of "ideal types."

While feudal relationships were governed by ideas of what individuals *are* or *do* to *one another*, monastic brotherhood was based on a common readiness of individuals to act as *instruments* of a supernatural power or purpose. When, for example, a knight was converted from a "vassal" to a "brother" (i.e. from being a man-of-another-man in a contractual exchange of benefice for service into being a member of an organization claiming unconditional devo-

CONCLUSIONS

tion), the basis of action shifted from self-seeking cooperation to self-sacrificing efforts. The same process in reverse would take place when a monk became a knight. But the fusion of active knighthood with monastic life in a single integrated role was quite another matter. It gave religious significance to military action, and military methods to religious action. Some elements of the monk role endowed the "knight" with the capacity to operate in a self-transcending ascetic and collectivistic organization; while some elements of the knight role endowed the "monk" with a capacity (and desire) to use power politically and activistically, instead of his past self-salvaging withdrawal from violence. ("They are joined in a peculiar union: they are at once meeker than lambs and more terrible than lions, so that one wonders whether they should be called monks or knights. They have the right to both names, for they possess the gentleness of the monk and the courage of the knight."—St. Bernard on the Knights Templars.)

It was a fundamental transformation of the previously separated and divergent roles, and it comprised a large segment of the knightly class, augmenting its size from various strata in a rather non-feudal social organization. How well this innovative role fusion suited the security needs of the Kingdom and prolonged its precarious existence was extensively described above. That feudal institutions were increasingly at a lag in relation to the changing international conditions was also sufficiently explained. It remains only to associate the institutional lag of the Jerusalemite feudalism with the new adaptational functions of the religio-military orders. Both the "lag" and the innovative role fusion were culturally rooted. But the congruence of these innovations with the previously separated monastic and knightly *ideals* did not imply congruence with the entrenched stratification system and political institutions. Thus the ensuing conflict between functional and culturally rooted *ideals* and disfunctional but institutionally supported *stratification system* indicates that power-status positions do not necessarily go hand in hand with adequate social leadership.

This is not to say that all institutional lags are caused by changing international systems, nor does it imply that all institutional transformations are accompanied by role fusions. It only points out that role fusion might be a form of social change, most probably under circumstances such as when conventional social leadership is in some crisis and when a discrepancy arises between new needs and culturally established positions of divergent social groups.

Characteristics of a Conflict System

It should be clear from the title of this item that it refers to a particular historical situation, not necessarily to a recurrent phenomenon. Yet it does not seem a marginal or exceptional occurrence in human history. Let it be, then, a historical type whose variations bring forth one or another of its basic themes.

1) The fundamental theme of the political culture of crusades and jihads was a radical denial of the enemy's right to coexist. As the conflict system evolved, the participant units were caught in an interlocking net compelling political leadership to conduct the affairs of state within a framework set by fanatical religious ideology. Avenues to cultural accommodation or regional affiliation were blocked by institutional compulsions to dominate the entire conflict system. Subjectively, the Holy War against the infidel was perceived in terms of *"malicidia"* (on the part of Christians) or "tearing up evil by the root" (on the part of Moslems). The escalation of the conflict directed both sides from the defense to the offense. Christians started with the limited objective of the "recovery of the holy places" and advanced toward destroying Islamic civilization at its centers. Moslems started with defensive jihads and in time recaptured the older idea of offensive jihads conducted by an ever-expanding caliphate. Most symbolic of this conflict system was the fact that the honor of slaying all Templar and Hospitaller prisoners (after the battle of Hittin) was

CONCLUSIONS

assigned by Salah-ad-Din to a unit of *Sufis* (a monastic-mystic fraternity) which performed it more enthusiastically than any regular soldiers would have. Sociologically speaking, the *Sufi* orders were the closest social form to the religio-military orders of Templars and Hospitallers.

2) As a transplanted small society, surrounded by hostile and numerically superior enemies (rather than as an outpost of Christendom encroaching upon Islam), the Kingdom of Jerusalem was persistently wavering between *political necessities* and *institutional compulsions* in the face of a total threat to existence. We shall formulate here these waverings by way of synoptical recapitulation of previous analysis:

—the need and opportunities to attract the various native Christians of the Levant to settle in town and country so that a sufficiently large Franco-Syrian society could meet the chronic manpower crisis of the Kingdom;

reluctance of the Roman Church to grant them equal religious status, combined with the institutional pattern of the Frankish nobility of establishing alien lordships over out-groups of villagers, craftsmen, and traders;

—the need and opportunities to develop maritime strength (both commercial and military) with the aid of interested and capable Italian settlers so that the Kingdom's income would be augmented, its military establishment buttressed, and a dense bourgeoisie would defend the coastal cities;

the fact that most Jerusalemite knights were themselves town dwellers and holders of money-fiefs rather than dispersed in rural castles prevented the formation of a socially segregated but politically strong urban bourgeoisie;

—the need for maximizing the frontier collectivistic colonization carried on by the religio-military orders which provided an unconditionally dedicated and self-sufficient standing army much superior to mercenaries and capable of tapping the European reservoir of proletarian knights as well as numerous pilgrims to the Holy Land;

CHAPTER 7

both the secular and ecclesiastic nobility were ambivalent to a movement which confronted (for the first time!) the feudal establishment with monks who were also powerful knights, and the regular clergy with a military organization possessing inherent religious authority; even the kings, who could hardly miss the vision of achieving a centralized and viable monarchy through the Orders, were naturally ambivalent to the prospect of a "theocratic revolution," and clung to customary feudal solidarity.

As was suggested before, a course of action which leads to a breakdown is no less "social change" than one resulting in "survival." It reflects a cultural detachment from an impinging reality; an incapacity to change in the face of a changing reality. Ultimately the developing international system brings about social change, one way or the other.

Characteristics of Inter-societal Systems

The following set of hypotheses is suggested as a guide for further investigation of the relationship between international relations and social change:

1) Societies exist in inter-societal environments which may be treated as systems, i.e. as wholes which determine, in a certain way, relations and functions of interdependent parts.

2) There are various types of historically evolved inter-societal systems which differ in structure and processes of change, but they all have some invariant common characteristics.

3) Inter-societal systems (although not culturally integrated as social systems tend to be) are based on a network of assumed positions (not "allocated") held by politically organized units, often constituting a problematic condition of existence to one another.

4) As the participants in an inter-societal system interact, their problems become functionally interlocked, and they tend to orient their institutions to one another; they establish patterns of communication (diplomacy), institu-

CONCLUSIONS

tionalized forms of conjunctive and disjunctive relations (alliances, protectorates, wars, truces, commercial treaties, etc.), and they hold dynamic role imputations with respect to one another.

5) Social institutions, whose general functions are to regulate man-to-man relations as well as man-to-environment adaptation, necessarily contain functions of inter-societal relations as part of social adaptation to environment. These latter functions may become a major determinant of internal stratification and of roles assumed by the power-status elite. Such functions and roles reflect the historically evolved political perspective as conditioned by changing modes of international existence.

6) Participants in an inter-societal system influence and modify one another's structure directly or indirectly. Direct changes are effected by various communications and interventions, from the diffusion of cultural elements to forceful intrusions.

Indirect changes result from balance changing factors (demographic, economic, military, technological, ideological, etc.) in parts of the inter-societal system, which induce adaptational or countervailing efforts in other parts of the system. Such exogenous influences may be referred to as induced functions of the international system, since they reflect the role played by one society in the structure of another.

7) Any new factor from the inter-societal system must be first "internalized" (perceived and integrated) by the responding unit, and then be "externalized" (reacted to and projected) in the cultural image of the concerned unit. Since internal power-status elites perform functions related to survival in inter-societal systems, their leadership positions within the units tend to correspond to inter-societal conditions. As the structure of the inter-societal system undergoes change so will the functions associated with political positions and with them the stratification system and the entire social order may be transformed. New groups may rise to power in order to readjust the political perspec-

tive. On the other hand, institutional rigidity due to internal vested interests or ideological resistance of the existing stratification system may be fatal with respect to survival.

8) Two alternative reactions to a changing inter-societal environment may be referred to as *institutional lag* and *innovative functions*. Institutional lag represents a persistence of action patterns adapted to needs of the past with respect to a changed inter-societal system, resulting in minimal adaptational consequences and a growing discrepancy between new needs and institutionally established functions. Innovative functions represent congruent or incongruent social innovations (relative to a given institutional order) resulting in optimal adaptational consequences with respect to problems arising in an inter-societal system. A potential transformation of social structure is implied thereby.

9) The entire series of historically evolved international systems must contain not only explanations of specific types, but also of change from one type to another and thus it comes to depend on variables taken from a general theory of social change, while the latter must draw significantly on knowledge of international relations.

Selected Bibliography

Atiya, Aziz, *Crusade, Commerce and Culture*, John Wiley & Sons, 1962.

Baldwin, Marshall W., *Raymond III of Tripolis and the Fall of Jerusalem* (1140-1187), Princeton Univ. Press, 1936.

Bloch, Marc, *Feudal Society* (trans. by L. A. Manyon), Univ. of Chicago Press, 1961.

Brundage, James A., *The Crusades, A Documentary Survey*, Marquette Univ. Press, 1962.

Cahen, Claude, *La Syrie du Nord à l'Epoque des Croisades*, Librairie Orientaliste Paul Geuthner, 1940.

Campbell, G. H., *The Knights Templars*, London, Duckworth, 1937.

Ganshof, François L., *"Le Moyen-Age"* (Vol. I) *Histoire des Relations Internationales*, ed. by Pierre Renouvin, Librairie Hachette, Paris, 1953.

Ganshof, François L., *Feudalism*, Harper, 1961.

Gibb, H.A.R., trans. of al-Qalanisi, *The Damascus Chronicle of the Crusades*, London, Luzel & Co., 1932.

Grousset, R., *Histoire des Croisades et du Royaume Franc de Jérusalem* (3 vols.), Paris, 1934-1936.

Heyd, W., *Histoire du Commerce du Levant* (trans. by Furcy Raynaud) (2 vols.), Leipzig, 1936.

Hodgson, Marshall G. S., *The Order of the Assassins*, Mouton & Co., 1955.

Hussey, J. M., *The Byzantine World*, Harper Torchbooks, 1961.

King, E. G., *The Knights Hospitallers*, Methuen, 1931.

LaMonte, John L., *Feudal Monarchy in the Latin Kingdom of Jerusalem*, Cambridge, Mass., 1932.

Lewis, A. R., *Naval Power and Trade in the Mediterranean* (500-1100), Princeton Univ. Press, 1951.

Melville, Marion, *La Vie des Templiers*, Gallimard, 1957.

Munro, Dana C., *The Kingdom of the Crusaders*, D. Appleton Century Co., 1935.

SELECTED BIBLIOGRAPHY

Oman, Charles, *A History of the Art of War in the Middle Ages* (2 vols.), Burt Franklin, 1953.

Paetow, Louis J., ed., *The Crusaders and Other Historical Essays*, F. S. Croft & Co., 1928.

Painter, Sidney, *A History of the Middle Ages*, Alfred A. Knopf, 1954.

Pernoud, Régine, *The Crusades*, Secker & Warburg, London, 1962.

Prawer, Joshua, *A History of the Latin Kingdom of Jerusalem* (2 vols.), Bialik Institute, 1963.

Richard, Jean, *Le Royaume Latin de Jérusalem*, Presses universitaires de France, 1953.

Runciman, Steven, *A History of the Crusades* (3 vols.), Cambridge Univ. Press, 1957 (includes a comprehensive bibliography of primary and secondary sources).

Setton, Kenneth M. and Baldwin, Marshall W., eds., *A History of the Crusades*, Univ. of Pennsylvania Press, 1958 (includes a comprehensive bibliography of primary and secondary sources).

Simon, Edith, *The Piebald Standard*, Little Brown & Co., 1959.

Smail, R., *Crusading Warfare*, Cambridge Univ. Press, 1956.

Stevenson, W. B., *The Crusaders in the East*, Cambridge, 1907.

Vasiliev, A. A., *History of the Byzantine Empire*, Univ. of Wisconsin Press, 1961.

William of Tyre, *History of Deeds Done Beyond the Sea* (trans. by Babcock and Krey), Columbia Univ. Press, 1943.

Wyman, W. D. and Kroeber, C. B., eds., *The Frontier in Perspective*, Univ. of Wisconsin Press, 1957.

Index

Abassid Caliphate, 30-33
Adhemar, Bishop, 28, 35-36
Al-Afdal, 34-35
Alexius Comnenus, 23-25
Alice of Antioch, 86-87
Amalric, King, 103, 113-17, 135, 137-38, 146, 164
Assassins, 154-55

Baldwin I, 36-41, 61, 65
Baldwin II, 42, 65, 67, 85
Baldwin III, 93-96, 101-102, 108-13
Baldwin IV, 161, 164-69
Baldwin V, 164, 168, 170
Bloch, Marc, 49, 180
Bohemond, 24, 36-37, 40
Bohemond II of Antioch, 166, 171
Byzantium, 23-26, 107-108; and Crusaders, 26; and Normans, 40; John's intervention in Syria, 89-93; Manuel's intervention in Syria, 110-11

Catholic Church, Roman, and First Crusade, 27-30; and Christian Syrians, 61-62
Christian Syrians, and Catholic Church, 61-62; and Crusaders, 61-62
conflict system, of Christians and Moslems, 184-86; and institutional compulsions of the Crusaders, 185
Constance of Antioch, 110
Crusade, First, and establishment of Christian principalities, 35-37; and Fatimid Egypt, 33-35
Crusade, Second, 94-98

Daimbert, 28, 65
diffusion, cultural, 6-7, 121-24
Durkheim, Emile, 5, 182

Egypt, Fatimid, 33-34, 102, 107-108; and First Crusade, 34-35; and Frankish and Syrian rivalry, 113-16; conquest by Syria, 117

feudal institutions, and Crusaders, 47-48; and institutional lag, 49, 74-75; and principalities, 52-54; and knightly class, 55-56
Fulk, King, 81, 85, 88-89, 91, 93

Genoa, and Crusaders, 26-27
Gerard of Ridfort, 163, 170, 172, 174, 176
Gerard of Sidon, 64-65, 135
Godfrey of Bouillon, 36-37
Gui de Lusignan, 166-72, 174, 176

Hart, Hornell, 11
Heraclius, Patriarch, 166, 176
historical sociology, 17-18
Hospitallers, 64-65, 68-71. *See also* religio-military orders
Hugh de Payens, 65, 67
Humphrey of Toron, 166, 169, 171

induced functions, and international system, 118-21, 158; and Holy Wars, 129-32; and prenationalism, 132; and centralization, 133-38; and feudal cooperation, 135; and the *assise sur la ligece*, 135-37; and religio-military orders, 138-45; and social change, 138-45, 178-80; definition of, 179; and international relations, 187
innovative functions, 49, 61-71, 74-75; and vassalage, 50-60; and Christian Syrians, 61-62; and maritime development, 62-64; and religio-military orders, 64-71, 74-75; and social change, 183-84; and international relations, 188
institutional lag, 49, 61-71, 74-75; and feudalism, 50-60; and Christian Syrians, 61-62; and

191

INDEX

maritime development, 62-64; and religio-military orders, 64-71; and feudal institutions, 74-75; and international relations, 188

international relations, as systems, 4, 71-72; and social structure, 8; and social change, 5, 9-14, 186-88; in Syria, 45-46; and stratification, 180-81, 187; and induced functions, 187; and institutional lag, 188; and innovative functions, 188

international system, 42-43; and induced functions, 118-21, 158; and the fall of Jerusalem, 175. *See also* inter-societal systems

inter-societal systems, 42-43, 76; and social structure, 71-76; and social change, 73-75, 179-80, 186; characteristics of, 186-88. *See also* international system

Isabel, Princess, 164, 169, 171
Italian naval powers, 38-39, 62-63

John, Emperor, 89-91
Joscelin of Edessa, 90, 93, 95, 163

Khaldun, Ibn, of Tunisia, 5
knightly class, 55-56

La Monte, John, 133
Latin Church of Jerusalem, 61; and Syrian Christians, 61-62

Malik-Shah, 31-32
Manuel, Emperor, 109-12
maritime development, 62-64
Marx, Karl, 12
Maudud of Mosul, 39, 41
Melisende, Queen, 85-86, 93, 95, 98, 101
Miles de Plancy, 137, 162
money fiefs, 125

Normans, 20-21; and Byzantium, 40
Nur-ad-Din, 77, 93-101, 103-105, 108-109, 111-13, 116-17, 121, 150-59

Ogburn, William, 10

Pareto, Wilfred, 5, 13
Pisa, and Crusaders, 26-27
Pons of Tripoli, 86-87
Pope Gregory VII, 24, 28
Pope Urban II, 25, 29

Raymond of Antioch, 92, 93, 95
Raymond of Toulouse, 36-37, 39
Raymond II of Tripoli, 92
Raymond III of Tripoli, 109, 113, 162, 164, 166-74
religio-military orders, 64-71, 138-47, 182-83; related to institutional lag and innovative functions, 64-71, 74-75; and social change, 64-71, 138-45; and induced functions, 138-45; and the Church, 163; and role-fusion, 64-65, 182-83. *See also* Hospitallers, Templars
Reynald of Châtillon, 64, 106, 108-11, 155, 163, 167-68, 170-71, 174, 176

Salah-ad-Din, 77, 117, 150-54, 162, 164-68, 170-74, 176
Saljuqs, 20-21, 30-33, 59-60
Shirkuh, 98, 113-17
Sibyl, Princess, 161, 164, 166, 170-71
social change, and external societies, 5; and diffusion, 6-7; and evolution, 6-7; and international relations, 9-14, 186-88; and the case of the Crusaders, 17; and religio-military orders, 64-71; and inter-societal system, 73-75, 179-80, 186; and induced functions (religio-military orders), 138-45; and role-fusion, 182-84; and innovative functions, 183-84
social structure, and international relations, 8; and inter-societal system, 71-76
Syria, 32-33, 41-43, 46; and international system, 42-43; and coalition of Moslems and Chris-

INDEX

tians, 43-44; and Byzantium, 89-93; Nur-ad-Din's conquest of Egypt, 117

Tancred, 36, 40
Templars, 64-71, 139-41. *See also* religio-military orders
transplantation, and social institutions, 15-16

Unur, Muin-ad-Din, 81, 83, 84, 96

Usamah, ibn Munkid, 84

vassalage, and institutional lag, 50-60; functions of, 127-28
Venice, and Crusaders, 26-27

Weber, Max, 12
White, Leslie, 6
William of Tyre, 116, 159-60, 166

Zangi, 45, 77, 79, 81-85, 89, 93

GPSR Authorized Representative: Easy Access System Europe - Mustamäe tee 50, 10621 Tallinn, Estonia, gpsr.requests@easproject.com

www.ingramcontent.com/pod-product-compliance
Lightning Source LLC
Chambersburg PA
CBHW051524230426
43668CB00012B/1731